D0540560

B

MAGAZINE

GUIDE TO THE

NATIONAL TRAILS

OF BRITAIN & IRELAND

◆

PADDY DILLON

David & Charles

Contents

Foreword

Paddy Dillon is one of those people for whom the comforts brought by twentieth-century technology seem but a mere inconvenience in the pursuit of walking challenges. Should you, having read this book, head off on a long-distance route and one day find yourself wet, lost and cursing Paddy's name, you can rest assured he's had a rougher time.

In researching these long-distance routes, Paddy has spent nights sleeping in ditches, wandering into an army road-block on the Northern Irish border and working his way home from one long-distance route by taking in another. Having worked with him over a number of years on *Trail Walker* magazine, he's always the man to give boots a really good test, or report on the longest trails. But not all long-distance walkers need suffer the hardships Paddy sets himself – unless of course you enjoy it.

Believe it or not, that's what long-distance walking is all about – enjoying it. Talk to legions of walkers halfway through a walk and they won't be too sure. But once they've met the challenge of finishing the whole route and quaffed a celebratory pint/half pint/tomato juice, then they'll be back for more.

David Ogle
Editor, *Trail Walker* magazine

Wanted: A Long Green Trail

Are you looking for a long green trail – one which you can follow for days across the verdant landscapes of Britain and Ireland? There are nearly two dozen official long-distance routes for walkers, covering over 3,700 miles (5,950km) of varied country. All of them are state funded, waymarked and promoted by a range of guidebooks. They will lead you through the Garden of England, the Larder of Scotland and the Orchard of Ireland. You can visit the place in Wales where St David was born, gaze on the spot where St George slew the dragon, or see where St Patrick drove the snakes out of Ireland. Legendary figures such as King Arthur and Fionn MacCumhail are encountered, as well as historical personages such as Captain Cook and William of Orange. You can break at the highest pub in England, or the oldest pub in Ireland, or visit the homes of Walter Scott or Daniel O'Connell; listen for the booming voice of the bittern on the Norfolk coast, or scour the Kerry countryside

for a glimpse of the rare spotted slug. Unusual plants such as St Patrick's Cabbage, the Spring Gentian, or St Dabeoc's Heath can be noted in the right quarters. Bleak bogs contrast with cultivated fields. Forests, mountainsides and broad downlands are passed. Some trails go through cities, towns and villages, then head for remote and unfrequented places. Broad tracks and narrow paths run beside rivers, lakes and the seashore.

Given the immensely varied countryside, unpredictable weather and seasonal variations, long-distance walking offers a kaleidoscope of colour, interest and experience. If you keep your eyes peeled you'll find free beer, free whisky, free money and a free foot-care service. You can spend your nights in opulent surroundings, or sleep under canvas. Spare time can be used to visit castles, museums, nature reserves or heritage centres – helping to broaden your understanding and experience of the countryside.

Walking near the rugged, granite headland of Bosigran Castle near Zennor

Making Trails

You could say that it all started on 22 June 1935. Tom Stephenson's article entitled 'WANTED: A LONG GREEN TRAIL' appeared in the *Daily Herald* on that date. 'Why should we not press for something akin to the Appalachian Trail?' he asked. 'A Pennine Way from the Peak to the Cheviots?' He imagined that the route would be 'a faint line on the Ordnance Maps which the feet of grateful pilgrims would, with the passing years, engrave on the face of the land.' Well, the engraving has gone rather deep in places, but there's no doubting that long-distance walking is becoming more and more popular.

It took thirty years of hard work to steer the Pennine Way to its official opening in 1965, but the ground was already being prepared for more trails. The Cleveland Way was declared open in 1969 and Wales had the Pembrokeshire Coast Path in 1970, followed by the Offa's Dyke Path in 1971. Throughout the 1970s, trails were blazed across the south of England. By 1980 the West Highland Way was the first trail to be designated in Scotland, and in the same year the Wicklow Way was opened in Ireland. The work continues through the 1990s – filling gaps in the enormous South West Way and Ulster Way, or preparing completely new trails for designation.

This guide looks at all the official trails which are planned, funded and maintained by various state agencies – the Countryside Commission, the Countryside Council for Wales, Scottish Natural Heritage, Cospoir and the Sports Council for Northern Ireland. These agencies often work in conjunction with local authorities and voluntary bodies. In England and Wales the routes are called 'National Trails', while in Scotland and Northern Ireland they are known as 'Long-distance Routes'. In Ireland they are termed 'Long-distance Walking Routes'. Some waymarked Irish routes are really only short day walks, so a lower limit of 60 miles (96km) ensures that only the real leg-stretchers are included.

Funding by state agencies has a number of benefits. First, the routes will have been carefully negotiated and should have no access problems. Second, the way should be marked and equipped with gates and stiles where necessary. Third, any problems arising with the trails should be addressed fairly promptly. Although the agencies may not produce guidebooks directly, it's likely that guidebook authors will have had some contact with them. Given that the official trails have a high profile, it's usually possible to find accommodation lists for each of them. Trails being developed for the future are listed in Appendix I. There are also some extremely popular unofficial trails such as the Coast-to-Coast Walk and the Dales Way. In fact, hundreds of trails have been in some way suggested, described in guidebooks or articles, or even waymarked on the ground.

The purpose of this guide is to allow you to compare and contrast the official trails in Britain and Ireland. By having each trail presented in a standard format, you'll easily be able to appreciate their scope, qualities, conditions and facilities. The text will tell you something about the areas they cover and a suggested daily schedule is offered. Don't worry if a daily stretch seems rather long, as a note will usually explain how you can make two shorter days of it. The route description is in outline form and is not intended to be used in the field. An information section lists more detailed guidebooks for each of the trails.

General Information

Waymarking

In England and Wales an acorn is the standard trail waymark symbol. In Scotland a thistle symbol is used. In all parts of Ireland a walking man symbol is standard. Usually, a yellow arrow will indicate the general direction, though other colours may be employed. In England and Wales, yellow arrows are usually used to denote footpaths, while blue arrows denote bridleways. More rarely, red or white arrows denote byways and permitted paths respectively. In Northern Ireland a high percentage of waymark arrows are orange. If you find arrows coloured black, green, etc, these don't denote any particular status. The name of the particular trail may be included on some signs and you might come across occasional bilingual signposts in parts of Wales and Ireland.

Schedules

The schedules break each of the trails into manageable daily stretches, which prospective walkers should adapt to suit their particular needs and abilities. It's not always necessary to cover 25 miles (40km) in a day, but sometimes you might have to cover in excess of 15 miles (24km) of quite rugged country. The schedules are built around the availability of indoor accommodation. If there's a handy youth hostel at the end of a day's walk, then YH is shown on the schedule. Independent hostels are shown as IH. If there is only bed and breakfast accommodation on offer, then BB is shown. Backpackers, of course, can either use trail-side camp-sites or negotiate for a pitch with any agreeable landowner. In some instances it might be possible to pitch discreetly in wild, remote places.

Maps

A standard scale of 1:50,000 is suggested throughout, to avoid 'map-lag' by constantly switching scales. In many cases you could use 1:25,000 maps, but this isn't available for every trail. The initials OSGB note maps which are published by the Ordnance Survey of Great Britain, covering England, Wales and Scotland. OSNI notes maps published by the Ordnance Survey of Northern Ireland, which covers Northern Ireland and adjoining parts of the Republic of Ireland. OSI notes maps published by the Ordnance Survey of Ireland, covering the Republic of Ireland. Not all the 1:50,000 maps quoted for the Irish trails have been published, so alternative Half Inch to One Mile maps are quoted also.

Guidebooks

A selection of detailed guidebooks are listed, so you can choose the type which suits your needs best. Some are full colour productions including Ordnance Survey maps – the National Trail Guide series. HMSO guides to Scottish trails come with specially produced Ordnance Survey maps. Other guidebooks may have excellent maps, basic maps, or no maps at all. Guidebooks which cover only part of the trails aren't listed. Some trails may be covered by simple folding leaflet guides. Although free leaflets are available for almost every trail, these aren't listed. They can be obtained from tourist information centres along particular trails, or direct from the appropriate state agencies concerned with the trails.

Accommodation Lists

Most trails have some sort of accommodation list. These vary greatly. Some show almost every camp-site, hostel, B & B or hotel on or near the trail. Others may be rather basic, or note only the places which have been approved by local tourist boards. The best are often produced by path associations. Some guidebooks may include accommodation details. Bord Failte has indicated that an accommodation guide will be available for all the Irish trails. There are annually updated hostel handbooks which give details of any hostels you might want to use. There's also the annual *Rambler's Yearbook and Accommodation Guide* which gives details of 'walker friendly' B & Bs as well as listing independent hostels. *Your Big Sites Book*, published by The Camping and Caravanning Club, lists hundreds of camp-sites in Britain and Ireland.

Path Associations

These associations consist of people who organise themselves to promote a particular trail, campaign on its behalf and disseminate information to potential trail users. Path associations can usually offer up to date route information and accommodation details. Most trails don't have a path association. Although the Irish trails often have a local committee, these are formed of a wide variety of groups whose main purpose is to negotiate and establish particular trails.

Tourist Information Centres

Sometimes, you'll need specific information about an area which neither your map nor guidebook can supply. Tourist information centres can often give you current details about local facilities, accommodation and public transport. Towns and villages on or near the trails which have such centres are listed. Addresses and telephone numbers always seem to change, so the best thing to do is to obtain the latest list – published in leaflet or booklet form on an annual, national basis. Don't expect tourist information centres to be able to offer route directions, though they may have useful publications on sale.

THE TRAIL NETWORK

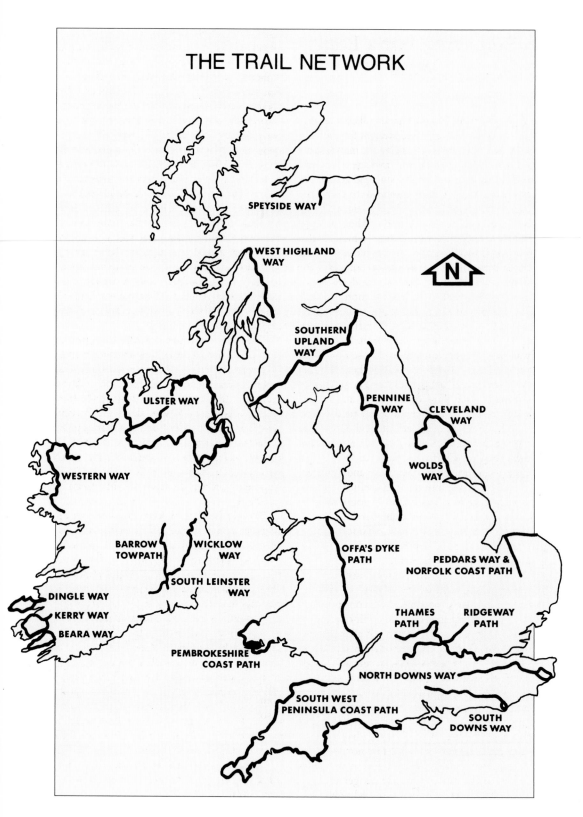

Preparing For a Long Walk

Experienced long-distance walkers may skip this section and head straight for the hills. Novices, however, should give the matter some thought. Most people can manage a 15 mile (24km) walk, but if you're stiff and aching the next day, then you might not want to repeat the experience again, and again, and again! Try a few weekend walks before tackling a long-distance trail. Choose a trail which you're confident you'll be able to complete. Novices on the Pennine Way tend to drop out within the first couple of days. Bear in mind that poor weather can make a long walk more difficult and blazing sunshine can make walking most uncomfortable. If you tend to suffer on steep hills, then choose a low-level trail. If you hate wallowing in peat bogs, then choose a trail with firm surfaces. Parts of the Southern Upland Way and several Irish trails have quite lengthy stretches along hard forest tracks and tarmac roads, where blisters could affect tender feet.

What you wear for walking will depend on the weather you're expecting for a particular time of year, as well as personal preference. Basically, you need to keep warm and dry when it's cold and wet, but it's also useful to be able to keep cool in a heatwave. On some trails, in good weather, you could walk in training shoes, but it's generally better to wear boots. Try to avoid heavy, unwieldy boots, but don't use anything flimsy if you want to keep your feet clean and dry. Spare clothing needs to be carried along with whatever else you take to ensure your walk is completed in comfort. Pack size and weight is largely determined by your choice of accommodation. Walkers using hostel or B & B accommodation can travel with lightweight packs. Backpackers will quickly weigh themselves down with a tent, sleeping-bag and cooking equipment. It's worth spending time and money trying to keep your pack as light as possible, without compromising comfort and efficiency. Long-distance backpacking can't really be recommended to novices, who should try the lifestyle over a few weekends before considering any of the longer trails.

Most walkers will choose a trail which will take them about a week or a fortnight to complete. Some of the shorter trails could be covered over a long weekend by determined walkers. The South West Way and Ulster Way are rarely covered in single expeditions. Most walkers seem to take an individual approach. Some walk alone, or take a dog, or a friend or two. Occasionally, a large group will tackle a trail and may even use a back-up vehicle for support. Although the ideal situation seems to be to walk a trail in one go, some walkers prefer to spread the load over several weekends, taking a year or more to cover a long trail. Some organisations offer guided walks along some of the more popular trails – making an expedition into something of a package holiday. There are no hard and fast rules, so you can please yourself how you plan and complete these trails. On some trails you'll be jostling alongside other walkers, but in some instances you may see hardly anyone else.

There are three books which illustrate the individual approaches of long-distance walkers on particular trails – all highly recommended:

One Man and His Bog, by Barry Pilton, published by Corgi, is an amusing and entertaining account of a walk along the Pennine Way. The humour is as black as a peat bog, but the author's wretched experiences would draw instant sympathy from anyone who has struggled along the same route. Why did he do it? Apparently, it was to stave off the effects of middle age.

500 Mile Walkies, by Mark Wallington, published by Arrow Books Ltd, is a humorous tale of a young man and a dog of considerable character tackling a walk around the South West Way. The author's honesty about his aches, pains and general incompetence is to be commended. Why did he do it? 'To impress a girl I met at a party before Christmas.'

Walking the Ulster Way, by Alan Warner, published by Appletree Press Ltd, is a more serious account of a walk around the Ulster Way. It's very good in respect of how advance planning can smooth your eventual passage on a long walk, and it should reassure walkers who would be worried to walk in that troubled province. Why did he do it? Simply to mark his retirement from work.

I don't know which trails you'll choose to walk, or how you'll choose to walk them, but I wish you well.

England

The South West Peninsula Coast Path

(map pp.24-5)

Commonly known as the South West Way, this is one of the longest waymarked trails. It may, or may not be as long as the Ulster Way. It was developed from the remains of old coastguard paths trodden out since the eighteenth century. Leisure walking arrived just in time to give these paths a new lease of life, as coastguards no longer tread regularly along the cliff tops and around the bays. Tales of smuggling and shipwrecks abound, and not all coastguards were paragons of virtue!

Look at a map of the south west of England and trace your finger round the coast from Minehead, in Somerset, to Poole, in Dorset. It's a crinkly coast which hides a considerable distance and so requires extra effort to complete. Then there are the relentless switchback sections, where rocky headlands are separated by deep, steep-sided combes. Bridges across several inlets can be some distance inland, so the South West Way makes use of a number of short ferries. It's not cheating – these are actually part of the route and help to maintain the coastal theme. All the ferries run in July and August, but outside of the peak season you might have to make detours around some inlets.

Distances vary from source to source, with quotes ranging from 500 miles (805km) to 600 miles (965km). The South West Way Association have a figure of 570 miles (917km), which seems reasonable. Note that any detours off-route for food and lodgings will increase the distance. The South West Way is really a summer expedition, when all the ferries are running, beach cafes are open and accommodation is readily available. Unfortunately, it's also a busy time and accommodation may have to be booked well in advance. Most walkers don't cover the whole distance in a single journey, but tend to tackle shorter stretches over a week or a fortnight. In fact, this trail has subdivisions which help walkers to consider particular lengths: the Somerset and North Devon Coast Path; the North Cornwall Coast Path; the South Cornwall Coast Path; the South Devon Coast Path; and the Dorset Coast Path. It all sounds quite a mouthful, but for the sake of clarity most signposts simply read 'Coast Path'.

The route starts in the Exmoor National Park and links every coastal Area of Outstanding Natural Beauty in the south west of England. Many stretches have been designated as heritage coasts, or national nature reserves. Parts are owned by the National Trust. With all this care and protection, it's just got to be good!

The schedule offered covers five weeks and is built around the availability of youth hostels. Gaps in the chain can be filled by using B & Bs, which are plentiful. There are also many coastal sites for backpackers. It's not necessary to carry large amounts of food as shops, cafes and pubs appear at frequent intervals. You may even begin to tire of all the Smugglers Inns and offers of cream teas. When you've got all your maps and guides together, the South West Way can seem a daunting prospect, but most stretches are fairly easy and you can keep the whole thing in perspective by treating the expedition as a series of day walks. If you lay your plans well you'll be able to enjoy the fascinating scenery, wildlife and history of the coast.

Highveer Point, where Exmoor falls steeply into the Bristol Channel

THE SOMERSET AND NORTH DEVON COAST PATH

Minehead to Lynton

20 miles (32km)

If your trek around the South West Way starts from Minehead Youth Hostel, then you'll have to walk some distance to reach the start of the walk. Little extras such as this increase the total distance. A signpost on the promenade says it's 500 miles (805km) to Poole. Don't believe a word of it – it's going to be much longer.

Zigzag up a steep, wooded rise to reach a heathery moor. The trail is a good step away from the sea and savours the flavour of Exmoor before hugging the coast more faithfully later. After passing close to 308m high Selworthy Beacon, a path goes down a steep combe almost to the sea, then turns inland to Bossington. A shingle bank leads from Bossington to Porlock Weir, where you can break for teas and snacks. The trail continues through woodlands to the small, secluded hamlet of Culbone. There's a small church here, with a refreshment hut nearby.

Landslips on the steep, wooded, seaward slopes have resulted in diversions inland. You must follow the re-routed trail even if it conflicts with information shown on your map and guide. It's a constant problem in some places, so be careful. While the route is away from the sea it passes from Somerset to Devon near the County Gate.

Steep slopes fall seawards and small streams run down wooded combes to the beaches. The coast path does not go round Foreland Point as a path on the far side is dangerous. After following a road steeply down to Lynmouth, an even steeper climb leads up to Lynton. There's a water-powered cliff railway to take weary walkers between the villages if required.

Lynton to Ilfracombe

18 miles (29km)

The narrow cliff path leaving Lynton is exciting, but safe and easy too. It leads through a gap to the Valley of the Rocks – a place of odd landforms. A road leads from Lee

Bay to Woody Bay, where a wooded path continues along the coast. You can later look back and see how precariously perched this path is. After turning round Highveer Point there's a descent into Heddon's Mouth. The Hunter's Inn lies a little way inland if a break is needed, or you can climb straight uphill to leave the valley.

A gentle path crosses Holdstone Down, then drops into Sherrycombe. Climb steeply out of the valley and head for a large cairn. This stands on the 318m summit of Great Hangman and is the highest point on the South West Way. The walk down from this point passes Little Hangman, and overlooks a rocky cove. Continue down to Combe Martin and look carefully for the course of the coast path – it's a fiddly route near a busy road, and don't go out onto

15

The Warren or you'll have to retrace your steps later.

A couple of minor headlands are passed on the way to Ilfracombe. Don't go straight into town, but climb the steep-sided Hillsborough first. A zigzag path leads to the 136m summit and there's a fine view over the town and its harbour. It's worth exploring the town's many nooks and crannies. The distant island which may be in view is Lundy. There are summer ferries to Lundy from Ilfracombe, but you'd need a whole day for a round trip.

Ilfracombe to Braunton

21 miles (34km)

If it wasn't for the River Taw and its estuary it would be possible to walk straight from Ilfracombe to the youth hostel at Instow. The Taw forces walkers inland to Barnstaple, which makes the distance to Instow rather too long. Unless you can organise some sort of ferry across the Taw, you'll have to stop at Braunton.

Follow the map and guide carefully, as it's easy to go wrong when leaving Ilfracombe. The Torrs Walk leads across Torrs Park, then a track away from the sea leads to Lee Bay and the village of Lee. A switchback route later takes the path round Bull Point and Morte Point, the latter featuring an attractive ridge of rock. After walking through the resort of Woolacombe, progress depends on the tide. Either walk straight across Woolacombe Sands or follow a track round the bay. A cliff path leads around Baggy Point to Croyde Bay, then the walk to Saunton is less attractive as it runs close to a road which can be busy.

Some walkers may take a short cut by road from Saunton to Braunton, but the coast path wanders between the dunes of Braunton Burrows and the levels of Braunton Marsh. You could go to the end of Crow Point and beg a boatman to take you to Instow or Appledore – a ferry once crossed the river here. If you're sticking to the walk, then follow the River Caen to Braunton to find a B & B for the night.

Braunton to Instow

13 miles (21km)

The River Taw is the first major estuary on the South West Way and it must be admitted that many walkers go round it by bus – even all the way from Braunton to Westward Ho! True, it isn't exactly coastal walking, but two level railway trackbeds have been pressed into service to keep you off the roads. These are combined walkway/cycleways and you cross the river between them at Barnstaple.

After leaving Braunton the route passes RAF Chivenor, the home base to some noisy jets. Simply follow the old trackbed to Barnstaple and cross the River Taw in this busy town. The railway paths, and parts of the coastal path, form the Tarka Trail – named after the novel *Tarka the Otter*. Notices highlight points of interest, but the scenery deteriorates near Instow. The youth hostel is a short way inland and uphill from the village. Remember to check the ferry and/or bus timetable for services to Appledore.

Instow to Clovelly

16 miles (26km)

If the ferry is operating, then use it to cross the River Torridge between Instow and Appledore. If not, then catch a bus round, or follow riverside paths and cross a high level bridge to reach Bideford. It's not really coastal walking and is an extra 6 miles (10km). Bideford has an all-year ferry service to Lundy Island. A path runs from Appledore to a point offering a view back to Braunton Burrows. It's been quite a detour around the Taw and Torridge, but true coastal walking resumes with a plod along a huge bank of shingle to reach the gaudy resort of Westward Ho! (It always has an exclamation mark and was named after the novel of that name by Charles Kingsley.)

A clear track continues along the coast where a low cliff line is attractive, but not particularly impressive. It's easy walking, but it becomes more difficult when narrow paths have to be followed across a rugged, wooded slope. After passing Buck's Mills, where there's a little shop, the path reaches The Hobby. This is another rugged, wooded area, but the broad Hobby Drive allows easy walking to the top end of Clovelly. An exceptionally steep, cobbled lane takes a nosedive to a tiny harbour. Clovelly is like an avalanche of cottages and although accommodation can be tight, this is the place to stay. Two trips up and down the main street would bring anyone to their knees!

Clovelly to Elmscott

14 miles (22km)

Apart from the climb out of Clovelly, the day starts with fairly easy walking through woodlands. Trees obscure a view of the sea, but there's a sudden, startling view down a cliff from Gallantry Bower. There are short, steep gradients around the rugged Mill's Mouth, then gentle cliff paths lead towards Hartland Point. The trail makes a significant turn at Hartland Point and the scene changes dramatically. In clear weather this is a testing walk through first class scenery. Rocky ridges, shattered stacks, high headlands, coves and combes offer sustained interest. In foul weather the walk would be very difficult. The monstrous switchback continues almost to Bude and the only point of refreshment actually on the route is the Hartland Hotel. Shortly after passing a fine waterfall at Speke's Mill Mouth, a short detour inland leads to Elmscott Youth Hostel – the last lodging on the Devon coast.

THE NORTH CORNWALL COAST PATH

Elmscott to Bude

10 miles (16km)

There's a fairly level cliff path near Elmscott, followed by a fearsome series of headlands and combes all the way to Bude. It's a short day in terms of distance, but it probably ranks as the hardest day's walk on the South West Way.

In this sort of country it's easy to lose track of all the ups and downs, but on entering Cornwall at Marsland Mouth the signposting becomes more helpful. Stout marker posts bear the names of most of the headlands and combes, so you can concentrate on the actual legwork. If you can take these gruesome gradients steadily, you should be able to enjoy the walk. The scenery is breathtaking – or is it just the effort? The cliffs and coves are all quite different and the terrain becomes easier towards Bude. This is an obvious place to break the walk, though you might want to continue further.

Bude to Boscastle

16 miles (26km)

Walk up to Compass Point and look back at yesterday's formidable cliff walk. Now it can be put behind and an easier part of the trail commences. Stay between a road and a low cliff line at Upton and Widmouth Bay. The cliffs increase in height and the road moves further inland. Rugged slopes at Dizzard are covered in impenetrable scrub, but the path keeps above it to pass by easily. A series of combes bite into the cliffs and shapely headlands are a feature of the walk to Crackington Haven. A series of ups and downs require some effort, but you can break for a snack at the Haven. Crackington Haven had an industrial past, dealing in coal, slate and lime. The rocky cove has a complex geology and colourful, contorted bands of rock can be traced across the cliff faces.

Keep a careful eye on the trail beyond Crackington Haven, as it's a bit fiddly in places. After walking around Beeny Cliff there's only a short walk onwards to Boscastle Harbour. Take your time and explore this curious, crooked inlet couched in a tight, rocky cleft. There's an air of secrecy about the place, but it's also popular with tourists. There's only space for a few buildings by the waterside and one of them is the youth hostel.

Boscastle to Port Isaac

14 miles (22km)

There's more to see of Boscastle Harbour at the start of the day's walk. A contorted cliff line has to be followed towards Tintagel, with lots of short ups and downs, ins and outs. Seaward views are enhanced by grotesque stacks, often colonised by birds. Walkers will doubtless be scanning every headland for a view of the legendary Tintagel Castle. It's an interesting place and has a fine situation regardless of whether King Arthur was born there or not. There's an exhibition centre, and you can pay to look at the ruins.

Continuing along the cliffs, the coast path passes a church and the solitary Tintagel Youth Hostel. Some might think that the splendid outlook from the hostel calls for an early halt, but others will wish to press onwards towards Port Isaac and a handy B & B for the night. The walk to Trebarwith Strand is fairly easy, but the way forward to Port Isaac is another switchback ride over headlands and combes. It isn't as hard as the trek from Hartland to Bude, but it does look vaguely similar. Taken steadily, it proves to be an enjoyable walk and you should spend time studying the tremendous gash of Barrett's Zawn. The final part of this cliff walk is an easy stroll between Port Gaverne and Port Isaac. Spend the evening exploring Port Isaac's poky little alleyways and quaint shops.

Port Isaac to Treyarnon

20 miles (32km)

A stretch of new coastal path was constructed in recent years between Port Isaac and Portquin. Whenever this happens, the South West Way invariably grows a bit longer. A stout fence and hundreds of steps ensure that you wander up, down, in and out on the correct line. Portquin lies at the head of a narrow inlet, then a series of coves and headlands occur. There are marked changes of direction along this contorted coast and the trail runs all the way round Pentire Point to reach the village of Polzeath.

The estuary of the River Camel forces a move inland, passing St Enodoc's Church on the way to the village of Rock. A ferry runs all year, except winter Sundays, from Rock to Padstow. This saves a lengthy walk round by way of Wadebridge, but be sure to check the ferry timetable in advance. Padstow is a delightful little town, well worth exploring, but keep an eye on the time as it's still a fairly long walk to Treyarnon.

It's not too far from Padstow to Treyarnon by road, but the coast path goes round Stepper Point and Trevose Head, which increases the distance. The cliffs are broken by sandy bays and there is an interesting blow-hole to study. The walking isn't difficult, but if you feel pushed for time you could short cut to Treyarnon.

Treyarnon to Newquay

13 miles (21km)

A complicated coast of cliffs and coves leads from Treyarnon to Porthtowan and Trenance. It's easy to lose track of exactly where you are, but there's no chance of going seriously astray. Don't go down via Pentire Steps or Bedruthan Steps as you'll find yourself on the beach and have to climb back onto the cliffs again. There are a series of attractive beaches on the way to Newquay, but walkers who wish to walk along them should be aware of the tides and escape routes. Anyone caught

by a rising tide at the foot of a cliff would have great difficulty trying to attract attention.

The cliff path reaches the outskirts of Newquay, but roads have to be followed through this busy resort. There's a youth hostel well before the town centre. Keep an eye on your map and guide as there are all sorts of distractions. If you walk out onto Towan Head in the evening you won't feel obliged to go there in the morning. You could also consider continuing to Perranporth.

Newquay to Perranporth

10 miles (16km)

There's an inlet called The Gannel which needs to be crossed between Newquay and Crantock. As this could cause a delay, the day's walking is kept fairly short. When the tide is out, there's a footbridge exposed across the river channel, but if the tide is in you'll have to use a seasonal ferry. If you know that the ferry isn't running, then you'll have to detour round to Crantock by road, incurring up to 5 miles (8km) extra walking.

The cliff paths around Pentire Point West and Kelsey Head are quite simple. After crossing dunes near Holywell there is a path round a military camp on Penhale Point. Keep seaward of a series of marker posts and enjoy views of the dramatic cleft island called Gull Rocks. The path around Ligger Point is more awkward and care is needed where it is perched above sheer cliffs. When the tide is out, the best way to Perranporth lies straight across the broad Perranporth Beach otherwise it's a tiresome plod across sand dunes. Explore the cliffs

around Perranporth, which have been cut by both the sea and the hand of man into strange formations. The youth hostel enjoys a splendid cliff top situation near the resort.

(*overleaf*) **A razor-edged ridge embraces a rocky cove near the village of Portreath**

f6 9142

Hurrying past Levant Beam Engine – a mining site owned by the National Trust

Perranporth to Gwithian

18 miles (29km)

Capped mineshafts lurk in the heather and bracken between Perranporth and St Agnes, then a series of ruined engine houses with brick chimneys come into view. Tin was hacked from tough granite until cheaper foreign sources killed the industry. Heather and gorse scrub cover the rugged slopes around Chapel Porth, where you could break at a beach cafe before tackling a steep climb uphill.

The cliff path between Porthtowan and Portreath is easy, but beyond Portreath there are a series of small combes to cross. The coastal scenery is impressive in places, then the trail runs close to a road on Reskajeage Downs, where thorny scrub is a problem. Deadman's Cove and Hell's Mouth sound rather grim and some twisted wreckage will be noticed on the rocks below. The coast path makes a circuit of Godrevy Head, offering views of Godrevy Island and its lighthouse. A road leads into the village of Gwithian, where limited B & B accommodation can be found.

Gwithian to Zennor

18 miles (29km)

Beyond Gwithian, extensive dunes rise from St Ives Bay, so it's easier to walk along the beach when tides allow. There is no ferry across the River Hayle, so a move inland is required. Hayle isn't a pretty village and it's mostly road walking to Lelant. The coast path roughly follows the railway to St Ives, but keep an eye open for waymarks, as some paths lead inland or to the beach.

Crowded streets and busy beaches may cause walkers to hurry through St Ives, but the town is well worth exploring first. It's also the last place to buy provisions unless you're prepared to make diversions inland before reaching Land's End. The path leaving St Ives runs into boulders and boggy patches. Switch-back sections start to develop and thorny scrub almost closes the trail in places. If the weather is good and you've energy to spare, then this is a fine stretch. If it's raining and you're tired, you'll find it a treadmill. Zennor, slightly inland, has a little B & B accommodation.

Zennor to St Just

12 miles (20km)

The coast path continues from Zennor, as before, with rocky headlands and coves. The scenery is excellent and the granite has weathered into huge blocks which look like ruined castles. Pay careful attention to your map and guide to keep track of the various features, though Pendeen Watch lighthouse is an obvious landmark.

Mining remains dominate the trail again and some are being rescued from ruin. There's a mining museum and Levant Beam Engine is worth visiting. Provisions can be bought by detouring inland to Pendeen, though there are a couple of invitations for cream teas near the path.

Various paths and tracks continue towards Cape Cornwall, which was once bestowed with all the accolades now claimed by Land's End. An old chimney points skywards from the cape and is a well-known landmark. Land's End can be seen and although it isn't far away it can wait until tomorrow. There's a youth hostel a short way inland near St Just.

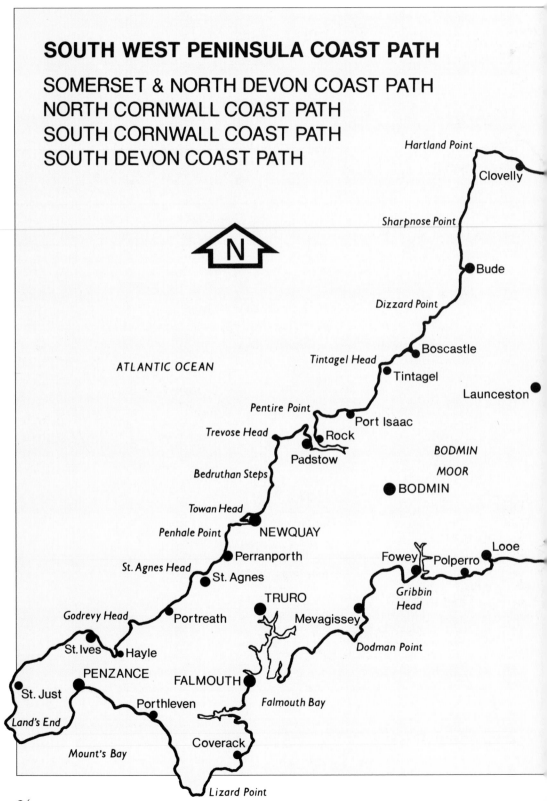

SOUTH WEST PENINSULA COAST PATH

SOMERSET & NORTH DEVON COAST PATH
NORTH CORNWALL COAST PATH
SOUTH CORNWALL COAST PATH
SOUTH DEVON COAST PATH

N

ATLANTIC OCEAN

Hartland Point
Clovelly
Sharpnose Point
Bude
Dizzard Point
Boscastle
Tintagel Head
Tintagel
Launceston
Pentire Point
Port Isaac
Trevose Head
Rock
Padstow
BODMIN
MOOR
Bedruthan Steps
BODMIN
Towan Head
Penhale Point
NEWQUAY
Perranporth
Fowey Polperro Looe
St. Agnes Head
St. Agnes
Gribbin Head
TRURO
Godrevy Head
Portreath
Mevagissey
St. Ives Hayle
Dodman Point
PENZANCE
FALMOUTH
St. Just
Porthleven
Falmouth Bay
Land's End
Coverack
Mount's Bay
Lizard Point

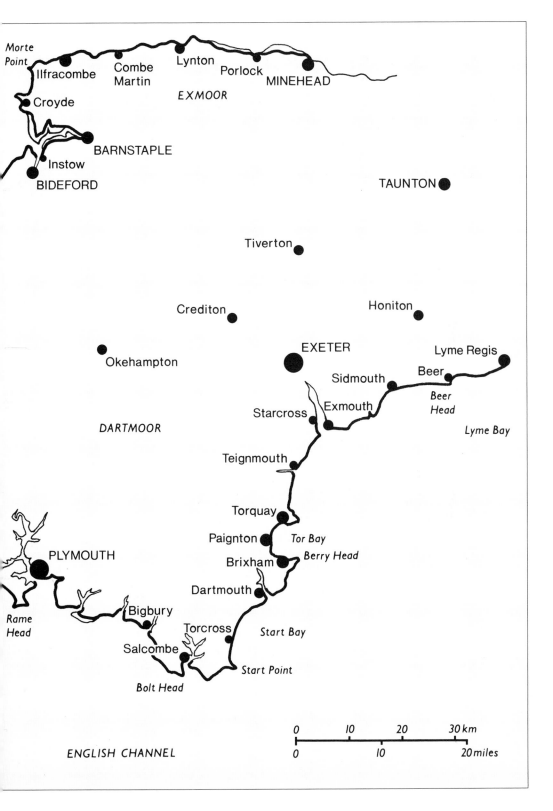

Morte Point

Ilfracombe

Combe Martin

Lynton

Porlock

MINEHEAD

EXMOOR

Croyde

BARNSTAPLE

Instow

BIDEFORD

TAUNTON

Tiverton

Crediton

Honiton

EXETER

Okehampton

Lyme Regis

Beer

Sidmouth

Starcross

Exmouth

Beer Head

DARTMOOR

Teignmouth

Lyme Bay

Torquay

Paignton

Tor Bay

Berry Head

PLYMOUTH

Brixham

Dartmouth

Bigbury

Rame Head

Torcross

Start Bay

Salcombe

Start Point

Bolt Head

ENGLISH CHANNEL

0	10	20	30 km
0		10	20 miles

DORSET COAST PATH

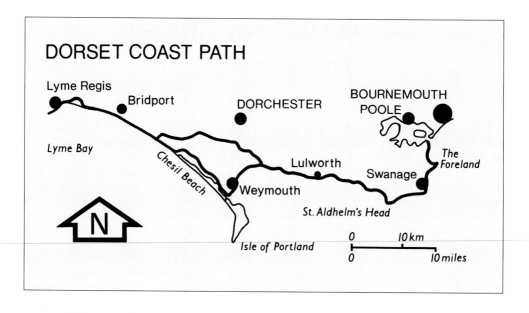

Lyme Regis

Bridport

DORCHESTER

BOURNEMOUTH
POOLE

Lyme Bay

Chesil Beach

Lulworth

Weymouth

Swanage

The Foreland

St. Aldhelm's Head

N

Isle of Portland

0   10 km

0   10 miles

St Just to Penzance

19 miles (31km)

The walk to Sennen and Land's End crosses some steep and rocky slopes, but the path is well worn and fairly easy. Sennen is the last village before Land's End, then the trail continues past oft-photographed scenes. There's the 'First and Last House', the celebrated signpost where you can have your picture taken, while behind the hotel a theme park has been built. You can turn your back on it all and look over blockish headlands to the Longships Lighthouse and the distant Isles of Scilly. The crowds are quickly left behind as the trail continues over headlands which are every bit as attractive as those at Land's End. There are plenty of short, steep ascents and descents, but nothing really difficult. Note the Minack Theatre, superbly sited on a cliff top, before a flight of steps leads to a rocky cove at Porthcurno.

The Logan Rock is situated slightly off-route, but is easily reached on a good path. This 80 ton boulder was pushed into the sea in 1824, and the culprit had to replace it on the headland! There's a short walk through woodland which seems out of character with the bleak and rocky headlands. After visiting the beautiful Lamorna Cove, where you could stop for a snack, the path clings precariously to the cliffs for a short distance. An easy track and road finally lead down to the charming village of Mousehole. As you pass the lifeboat station you're reminded of the disaster in 1981 when the crew were lost at sea. There is no coast path through Newlyn and Penzance, so the road has to be followed. Penzance has a youth hostel and the best range of services for some time.

THE SOUTH CORNWALL COAST PATH

Penzance to Mullion

20 miles (32km)

The walk around Mounts Bay is easy, but begins with a dull stretch. Follow the road out of Penzance, then use a sandy path on the seaward side of the railway. This leads to the ancient village of Marazion. St Michael's Mount rises from the sand or sea, depending on the state of the tide. You'll need plenty of spare time if you want to include a visit to the Mount.

Landslips beyond Marazion have resulted in a path diversion, so keep an eye open for waymarks. There is also a fiddly section around Perranuthnoe. A low cliff line is followed around Cudden Point to Prussia Cove and on to Praa Sands. If the tide permits, walk straight across Praa Sands to join a cliff path leading round Trewavas Head. The path can be difficult in places. There are odd ruined tin mines clinging to the cliffs, but these reminders of former industry are becoming scarcer.

Porthleven has a sheltered harbour, but a substantial buttress protects the seaward part of town. The Loe and Carminowe Creek were once tidal inlets, but the sea has heaped up a huge bank of sand and shingle across the river mouths. Walk along the bank, which is called Loe Bar, between two low crumbling cliffs. The coast path moves on to Gunwalloe Fishing Cove – which has seen better days. The cliffs beyond the cove are intricate and interesting. Sandy coves on the way to Mullion are quite popular and Mullion Cove is a delightful secret harbour lodged in a deep, rocky cleft. Seaward views are full of stacks. Lodgings are available nearby.

Mullion to Coverack

15 miles (24km)

Lizard Point is Britain's most southerly point. Its hinterland is a low plain, but the cliff edges are cut by a number of steep-sided ravines. The walk from Mullion to Lizard Point is fairly easy as all the ascents and descents are quite short. The Lizard is roughly the halfway point on the South West Way and you could break at a cafe to celebrate. Seals are common offshore, with dolphins being infrequent visitors.

Note the greenish rock called serpentine which occurs locally and is made into ornaments. The banded rock is soft and takes a high polish, so it can be slippery when wet. Walking away from the Lizard, there are some minor switchbacks to be negotiated on the way to Cadgwith. Just before this charming village is the Devil's Frying Pan – a curious hollow excavated by the sea. The country beyond Cadgwith can be difficult. There are plenty of ups and downs, which take some effort, but there is also abundant thorny scrub which almost closes the trail. Be prepared to lose some blood before reaching Black Head. The land levels around Black Head and the scrub falls back from the path. Progress towards Coverack is much easier. There is a youth hostel at the top end of the village.

Coverack to Falmouth

20 miles (32km)

Quarries spoil some of the walking beyond Coverack. There is a marked route through one quarry, but no access to the next one. It's necessary to detour uphill and inland before descending to Porthoustock. Old quarries further along the coast are avoided and the coast path moves inland again before reaching Porthallow. A good path goes round Nare Point and heads for Gillan. The inlet at Gillan Harbour can be crossed while the tide is out to allow walkers to reach St Anthony. If the tide is in, you can either walk round to St Anthony by road, or cut a corner and go straight to Helford.

The Helford River is a major inlet with only a seasonal ferry. Check the dates and times of operation in advance. Even then, you'll have to open a special sign to call the ferry across. The coast path continues from Helford Passage, with fairly gentle walking along low cliffs and around wooded bays. After passing the villages of Durgan, Mawnan and Maenporth, the outskirts of Falmouth are reached. It's possible to head straight for the town centre, but it's better to walk round Pendennis Head first. There is a youth hostel on top of the headland, in Pendennis Castle. Check the ferry timetable for tomorrow, then you'll know how much time you can spare for exploring Falmouth in the morning.

Falmouth to Boswinger

17 miles (27km)

The day begins with two ferry journeys. The ferry from Falmouth to St Mawes runs all year, except for winter Sundays. This saves an enormous detour to the nearest bridge at Truro. Have a look around St Mawes. The village isn't really on the South West Way, but is simply a stepping-stone between two ferries. A small seasonal ferry runs across the Percuil River from St Mawes to Place.

The coast path begins again, running from Place to St Anthony Head, with views across to Falmouth and Pendennis Head. A fairly simple path leads along a pleasant cliff line to Portscatho. The route to Pendower is also easy, though pitched on a rather steep slope. The walk around Gerrans Bay ends with a climb onto Nare Head, then the trail becomes more difficult. There are coves and headlands to traverse on the way to Portloe and some gradients are steep.

Portloe is an attractive huddle of buildings around a small harbour and there are just enough facilities to satisfy a tired, hungry, thirsty walker. An easy cliff path leads towards Portholland, then paths and tracks continue towards Porthluney Cove, ending with a view of Caerhays Castle. Climb onto the next cliff line and head towards Hemmick Beach, where a short detour inland leads to Boswinger Youth Hostel.

Boswinger to Fowey

22 miles (35km)

The circuit of Dodman Point is completed easily in the morning. It's quite a shapeless headland, but once you've walked round it you'll be able to pick it out in distant views for some time. The 114m summit bears a stout, stone cross. The whole day's walk is made up of circuits around rugged headlands and bays. After visiting Gorran Haven the coast path heads around Chapel Point. It's not possible to go right to the end of the point, which is private. The villages of Porthmellon and Mevagissey are followed by a walk out onto Penare Point.

The walking throughout the day is fairly easy, but it has its rough and tough moments. Beyond Pentewan there are some minor ups and downs, then a fine walk leads onto Black Head. There are steep gradients beyond, and some awkward route finding on the way to the industrial harbour at Charlestown. Walking around St Austell Bay is uninspiring. Holiday camps and houses are near the path, a grubby china clay works, then a road and railway have to be passed. Only the odd glimpse of Gribbin Head promises better things to come.

Portloe is just one of many charming, cluttered villages on the coast path

The walk out to Gribbin Head is easy, then the route becomes more convoluted on the way to Fowey. There is plenty of accommodation in town, but the youth hostel is further inland. If you're staying there, you'd probably find it best to get a taxi there to avoid further walking at the end of this long day.

Fowey to Portwrinkle

18 miles (29km)

Regular ferries ply across the mouth of the River Fowey all year and quickly convey walkers to Polruan. There are poky alleyways and quaint corners in both Fowey and Polruan. The trail starts easily, but quickly becomes involved in a series of little headlands and combes, with their attendant ascents and descents. Landmarks are few on this stretch, but a solitary building gives away the position of Polperro – a large village which otherwise breaks suddenly into view.

Polperro has a complex harbour which forces walkers well into the busy centre of town. After squeezing through the narrow streets, easy walking continues around a couple of headlands and bays. Seaward views feature Looe Island, otherwise known as St George's Island, then the town of Looe which comes in two parts, West and East, with a river in between. There's a bridge linking the two halves, or you could save a couple of minutes by taking a short ferry ride. Looe is worth exploring if you've any time left after visiting Fowey, Polruan and Polperro.

The coast path runs beside houses until it's clear of Millendreath Beach, then it takes to a wooded slope below the Murrayton Monkey Sanctuary. Seaton isn't a pretty place, with its rather grim, grey beach. A road leads through Downderry, but the way out of the village isn't too clear. Keep an eye on the map and guide to reach Portwrinkle, which has B & B accommodation available.

Portwrinkle to Plymouth

17 miles (27km)

Leaving Portwrinkle, the trail moves inland to avoid firing ranges near Tregantle Fort. An effort has been made to keep walkers off the road, but a road has to be followed back to the coast at Freathy. An awkward series of paths weave between chalets which are arranged haphazardly on a steep slope. The overall effect looks like a terrible landslip carrying a village into the sea. When the chalets are left behind, a more direct path makes a beeline towards Rame Head. The coast path doesn't go onto the actual headland, but there's an ancient chapel you might want to visit and this is as close as you'll get to the famous Eddystone Lighthouse.

An easy path leads around Penlee Point, then good tracks and paths continue to Kingsand. If you know you can make the last ferry of the day, then press on to Cremyll. Easy paths and tracks lead through Mount Edgcumbe Country Park – an area of woods, gardens and strange follies. A ferry runs all year between Cremyll and Plymouth. This is the only city on the South West Way and it has a tremendous naval history. Although the place was almost levelled during the war, The Hoe and Barbican are two remaining points of antiquity you can visit. There is a youth hostel in Plymouth and the city has the fullest range of facilities along the entire walk.

THE SOUTH DEVON COAST PATH

Plymouth to Bigbury

21 miles (34km)

The walk from Plymouth to Turnchapel is one of the least inspiring parts of the South West Way. There used to be a ferry to Turnchapel, and walkers could do themselves a favour by catching a bus there. The trail still has to pass holiday chalets and a firing range before the scenery improves at Wembury. The walking is easy, but it mustn't make you complacent. It might not even be possible to reach Bigbury and you'll have to make a decision whether to continue.

The tidal inlet of the River Yealm is the first obstacle. This has a very limited summer service. Even then you have to walk down the Ferry Steps, yell 'Ferry' and hope for the best. You can take this ferry to Newton Ferrers if you opt for an early B & B, or to Noss Mayo if you decide to press on towards Bigbury.

An easy, well-graded track leads around the coast. Again, keep thinking ahead as there is another obstacle. You can buy a few provisions from a small shop at a camp-site in the summer, in case you get stuck later. When the track ends there are some steep ups and downs before the wooded mouth of the River Erme is reached. There is no ferry across this inlet and the nearest bridge is far inland. With no handy accommodation, you must wait until the tide is out and cross between two marker posts.

Once across the Erme, the final stretch to Bigbury is quite difficult. Huge, steep-sided combes cut the cliff line and you'll need plenty of time and energy to complete the trek. The scenery is stunning and the sea is full of sharp stacks, but the path runs close to a crumbling edge and needs care. There are lodgings in Bigbury, and an hotel on Burgh Island which you could reach on foot at low water.

Bigbury to Salcombe

13 miles (21km)

The day begins with a short walk and a short ferry. The ferry has only a limited summer schedule, so check it in advance. It runs between a shingle bank called the Cockleridge and the lovely village of Bantham. The River Avon is charming hereabouts, but a bit too deep and dangerous to cross on foot at low water.

The coast path is easy all the way past Thurlestone and around the bay to the twin villages of Outer Hope and Inner Hope. It's a good idea to break for a snack before walking from Bolt Tail to Bolt Head, though there is an hotel near the trail which could be visited later. Fairly rugged paths lead towards Bolt Head and the cliff line is highly contorted, so that there are many fine headlands and narrow coves. Fine rocky edges and tottery tors add character and interest to the walk and although several paths cut across the rugged slopes, it doesn't matter if you take the wrong one.

After rounding Bolt Head the path descends into Starehole Bay, then climbs up stone steps around the shattered Sharp Tor. The scenery is outstanding and the sea usually features plenty of boats. Hostellers should pay particular attention to their map and guide, as the hostel is situated above the trail before reaching South Sands. A steep, narrow road links South Sands with Salcombe. If this is busy with traffic you could use a seasonal ferry to reach Salcombe instead.

Salcombe to Dartmouth

20 miles (32km)

The ferry across Salcombe Harbour, from Salcombe to East Portlemouth, runs all through the year. The walking is easy at first, but there are rugged slopes ahead and fine cliffs on the way to Prawle Point. This is the most southerly point in Devon and it seems to have more snakes and lizards than anywhere else you could walk. After turning Prawle Point the coast path traces a low crumbly edge near the sea, while fields rise gently to the foot of a cliff line further inland. Start Point marks a significant turn, revealing a view along a great shingle bank, Slapton Sands, curving round Start Bay.

Hallsands is a well known ruined village which was wrecked by storms after offshore dredging destroyed its protective bank of shingle. Beyond Hallsands are Beesands and Torcross. Clay cliffs are crumbling hereabouts, so expect diversions. The bank of shingle around Start Bay has sealed off a couple of large pools on the landward side – the largest being Slapton Ley. The coast path runs close to a busy road, while beyond Strete Gate there is no option but a road walk to Stoke Fleming. A path beyond Stoke Fleming leads back to the coast and passes crinkly headlands on the way to Dartmouth. This naval town is well worth exploring and has plenty of accommodation.

Dartmouth to Torquay

19 miles (31km)

There are three ferries across the mouth of the River Dart, two of which link Dartmouth with Kingswear all year round. It's not immediately apparent where you should aim to leave Kingswear, so have your map and guide ready. The coast path uses a road, tracks and paths to go round wooded headlands. On emerging from the woods, you'll need plenty of energy to reach distant Brixham. Little combes and headlands are followed by much sterner ascents and descents; then the way becomes easier at Sharkham Point.

The suburbs of Brixham impinge on the trail, but don't head for the town until you've visited the large fortresses on Berry Head. These were built in response to Napoleonic invasion threats, but now house a wildlife centre and a cafe. Head straight down to Brixham and have a look round the town and its harbour. There are many features of interest, such as a replica of the Golden Hind and a statue marking the landing of William of Orange.

Some walkers look on the Torbay resorts as a blackspot, but the walk from Brixham to Goodrington is quite scenic and the promenade walks through Paignton and Torquay aren't too bad. Even so, some folk simply catch a bus through the area. If you're tempted to do that, consider instead using the seasonal ferry across the bay, allowing a more distant view of the 'English Riviera'.

Torquay to Exmouth

16 miles (26km)

Torquay is built on an impressive headland and there is generally enough room for the coast path to squeeze between the hotels and the cliffs. Follow your map and guide carefully, as it's not as simple as it sounds. Beyond Babbacombe there are a series of ups and downs. There's also a cliff railway, but this is of no use to walkers seeking an easy option. The undulations are fairly short in pitch, but can be tiring when all the ups and downs come in quick succession. Maidencombe appears half-way if you need a break.

Crossing Salcombe Harbour, which is often very busy with pleasure boats

Eventually, you'll reach Shaldon and can look across the River Teign to Teignmouth. A bridge links the two places, but there is also a ferry operating throughout the year which saves a short walk and a few minutes. There's no official trail out of Teignmouth, but, if the tide allows, you could follow the sea wall beside the railway. There's a tunnel under the railway allowing access to Holcombe, but this floods with the tides. After the detour inland to Holcombe, the railway is followed from Dawlish to Dawlish Warren – from a pleasant little resort to a holiday camp. A road walk continues to Starcross, where a seasonal ferry crosses the estuary of the River Exe to reach Exmouth.

Exmouth to Beer

19 miles (31km)

The way out of Exmouth is along the promenade, through a holiday park, then over a rugged, reddish cliff line to reach the genteel resort of Budleigh Salterton. The River Otter cuts across a shingle bank to reach the sea, forcing walkers slightly inland to cross a bridge. Easy walking leads to Ladram Bay. This is an attractive area with large, red stacks rising from the bay. A climb up High Peak is followed by Peak Hill. These ascents aren't difficult and the route misses the actual summits. A promenade walk leads through Sidmouth and you might want to break for a while before tackling the next part of the trail.

The high cliffs between Sidmouth and Beer are cut by deep, steep-sided combes. The coast path keeps climbing to over 150m, only to plunge back to sea level again. Salcombe Mouth, Weston Mouth and Branscombe Mouth are the low points, while the actual cliff tops between them are quite level. There's food and drink at Branscombe Mouth, then a climb onto Beer Head. This is quite interesting as the path climbs up through a landslip. There are chaotic landforms covered in scrub, then a final pull to the top of the headland. An easy walk leads down to Beer, which has a youth hostel.

THE DORSET COAST PATH

Beer to Bridport

20 miles (32km)

A simple, easy, but exciting little cliff path leads from Beer to Seaton. A move inland is required before the edge of Haven Cliff can be reached. The South West Way suddenly plunges over the edge of the cliffs and enters an area known as the Undercliff. This is a rugged area of large landslips covered in a jungly scrub. A clear trail threads its way through this strange place and you're largely committed to it all the way to Lyme Regis.

Halfway through the day's walk the trail switches from the South Devon Coast Path to the Dorset Coast Path. Lyme Regis has plenty of fine buildings and a large number of fossil shops, Lyme Bay being a palaeontologist's paradise. Walkers, however, may be disappointed at the enormous detour inland to avoid a series of landslips. This is a common occurrence along the Dorset coast. The shore is regained at Charmouth.

The switchback route from Charmouth to Bridport is slowly moving inland as sections of the low cliffs fall into the sea. The undulations increase in height, then there's a stiff little climb onto Golden Cap – a 191m high summit which is the highest on the English Channel. After descending to Seatown, some of the succeeding humps can be bypassed by following paths around their flanks. Press onwards to cross West Cliff on the way to West Bay, then move a little way inland to reach Bridport, which has a youth hostel.

Bridport to Weymouth

23 miles (37km)

It's a long day's walk, but fairly easy going for the most part. There is a short, but very steep climb onto East Cliff, then another climb onto Burton Cliff. These ascents offer good views along the immense shingle bank of Chesil Beach to the distant Isle of Portland. The South West Way follows this great bank at first, but you'll find that it's hard work. Curiously, the pebbles are graded from bean-sized near Bridport to potato-sized near Weymouth. Speaking of food, there's a beach cafe at West Bexington if you need a break.

At West Bexington there's also the beginning of an inland alternative to the coast path called the Dorset Ridgeway. This completely bypasses Weymouth and saves some distance by following paths and tracks across the downs instead of around the coast. However, it would be a pity to abandon the coastal theme at this late stage, and Weymouth isn't that bad, so continue along the pebbled ridge. There's a move inland around Chapel Hill near the Abbotsbury Swannery, where Chesil Beach encloses a stretch of water called West Fleet. The trail runs through fields, past Clayhanger Farm to Wyke Wood, then heads for the shore of East Fleet. There's a hotel along the way if you need food and drink.

A firing range beside the East Fleet might require a detour, then a military depot also causes a move away from the water's edge. Despite the easy nature of the day's walk, the distance is high and walkers might feel inclined to stop at the first B & B. Alternatively, continue into the centre of Weymouth to take advantage of a greater range of services.

Weymouth to Lulworth

12 miles (19km)

After yesterday's long walk, you can relax a little on today's walk. There should be time to explore Weymouth before leaving, but don't dawdle as there is more difficult walking ahead. Follow the promenade out of Weymouth to Bowleaze Cove, then trace a crumbling cliff line until a detour is marked inland. The coast is reached at Osmington Mills, where the Dorset Ridgeway also ends.

Some easy walking follows, but the path beyond Ringstead Bay embarks on a strenuous switchback over chalky headlands and combes. Sheer cliffs fall spectacularly to the sea and there's even better to come. Durdle Door, Stair Hole and Lulworth Cove are fascinating places formed where the sea has broken through a resistant band of rock and worn away the softer chalk. The pierced headland of Durdle Door is very popular, as is Lulworth Cove. At Stair Hole you can witness the process of erosion which ultimately led to the formation of Lulworth Cove. There's a youth hostel slightly inland at West Lulworth. It's a good idea to check the state of the firing ranges which cover the next part of the route. It would be a pity to mistime this part of the trail and be deprived of some of the finest scenery.

Lulworth to Swanage

20 miles (32km)

Just when you think the end of the walk is near, you're faced with one of the sternest day's walks on the South West Way. First, you've got to be sure that there's no firing on the Lulworth ranges – between Lulworth Cove and Kimmeridge Bay. Many weekends and holiday periods are available to walkers, and once inside the ranges you should stick to the marked trail.

Apart from the steep climb around Lulworth Cove, the first part of the day's walk is quite easy. Steep climbs occur above Mupe Bay and Worbarrow Bay. After crossing the overhanging Gad Cliff, the coast path just misses the summit of Tyneham Cap. A good track leads off the range close to a 'nodding donkey' oilpump at Kimmeridge Bay. Slabs of rock surround the bay and a far headland is crowned with a ruined tower. You may be able to get an ice-cream around here, but you won't find anything else until the end of the day's walk.

The coast path continues fairly easily for a while, but becomes more difficult with a steep pull over Houns-tout Cliff. The trail moves inland to cross a valley. The way to St Aldhelm's Head is mostly easy, except for a sudden, steep ravine which has to be crossed by steps. Once on the headland the stout, stone St Aldhelm's Chapel can be inspected.

There is some rugged walking beyond St Aldhelm's Head to Swanage, but this is tempered by easier stretches. The cliff line is fairly low, but also highly complex. Look for undercut edges, large holes and tilted slabs – all part of a series of quarries, some of which were worked from the sea. A choice of high or low level paths lead towards a lighthouse and the coast path turns around Durlston Head. A wooded walk leads to Peveril Point, then a final turn leads into Swanage. There is a youth hostel in the town and a number of interesting places to visit.

Swanage to Poole Harbour

7 miles (11km)

An easy day to finish the walk along the South West Way. The walk around Swanage Bay continues over Ballard Cliff and out to the end of The Foreland. This chalky point has been broken into huge stacks known as Old Harry's Rocks. Distant views look towards The Needles and the Isle of Wight.

The trail ends with less scenic merit. After following a good track towards Studland, go down to the beach. The walk around Studland Point is easy if the tide is out, but could be difficult if you're pushed onto the dunes. This is a nude bathing area, so you may feel overdressed in your shorts and teeshirt! Turn around South Haven Point, walk to a road end and catch the next ferry across the mouth of Poole Harbour. The walk is over and the next bus will take you to Poole or Bournemouth.

SOUTH WEST PENINSULA COAST PATH INFORMATION

Schedule:	*miles*	*km*
Minehead – Lynton YH	20	32
Lynton – Ilfracombe YH	18	29
Ilfracombe – Braunton BB	21	34
Braunton – Instow YH	13	21
Instow – Clovelly BB	16	26
Clovelly – Elmscott YH	14	22
Elmscott – Bude BB	10	16
Bude – Boscastle YH	16	26
Boscastle – Port Isaac BB	14	22
Port Isaac – Treyarnon YH	20	32
Treyarnon – Newquay YH	13	21
Newquay – Perranporth YH	10	16
Perranporth – Gwithian BB	18	29
Gwithian – Zennor BB	18	29
Zennor – St Just YH	12	20
St Just – Penzance YH	19	31

Penzance – Mullion BB	20	32
Mullion – Coverack YH	15	24
Coverack – Falmouth YH	20	32
Falmouth – Boswinger YH	17	27
Boswinger – Fowey BB	22	35
Fowey – Portwrinkle BB	18	29
Portwrinkle – Plymouth YH	17	27
Plymouth – Bigbury BB	21	34
Bigbury – Salcombe YH	13	21
Salcombe – Dartmouth BB	20	32
Dartmouth – Torquay BB	19	31
Torquay – Exmouth BB	16	26
Exmouth – Beer YH	19	31
Beer – Bridport YH	20	32
Bridport – Weymouth BB	23	37
Weymouth – Lulworth YH	12	19
Lulworth – Swanage YH	20	32
Swanage – Poole Harbour BB	7	11
Total distance	571	918

Maps:
OSGB 1:50,000 Landranger Sheets 180, 181, 190, 192, 193, 194, 195, 200, 201, 202, 203 & 204.

Guidebooks:
National Trail Guides, South West Coast Path, Minehead to Padstow, by Roland Tarr, *Padstow to Falmouth*, by John Macadam, *Falmouth to Exmouth*, by Brian Le Messurier, *Exmouth to Poole*, by Roland Tarr, all published by the Countryside Commission, Ordnance Survey and Aurum Press Ltd. *South West Way, Minehead to Penzance, South West Way, Penzance to Poole*, both by Martin Collins, published by Cicerone Press. *South West Way*, by the South West Way Association, an annual update published by Peninsula Press.

Accommodation List:
The South West Way Association.

Path Association:
The South West Way Association.

Tourist Information Centres:
Minehead, Lynton, Combe Martin, Ilfracombe, Woolacombe, Braunton, Barnstaple, Bideford, Bude, Padstow, Newquay, Perranporth, St Ives, Penzance, Falmouth, Fowey, Looe, Plymouth, Dartmouth, Brixham, Paignton, Torquay, Teignmouth, Dawlish, Budleigh Salterton, Sidmouth, Seaton, Lyme Regis, Bridport, Weymouth, Poole, Bournemouth.

The South Downs Way

(map pp.44-5)

When the South Downs Way was opened it was heralded as the first long-distance bridleway and it ran from Eastbourne to Buriton. In recent years it's been extended to Winchester. Although horse riders and cyclists can use the whole of the route, walkers are more numerous and, because it's a bridleway, there are gates which open easily if you get tired of climbing stiles.

The seaward end of the South Downs Way, around Eastbourne, Beachy Head and the Seven Sisters, is very popular. Inland, there are busy places such as Ditchling Beacon, Butser Hill and Old Winchester Hill. The central, largely wooded stretches are quieter, but the South Downs Way is so gentle that you could expect to meet other walkers at any point throughout the year. The route runs from the Sussex Downs Area of Outstanding Natural Beauty to the East Hampshire Area of Outstanding Natural Beauty and the seaward end has been designated a heritage coast. From time to time there have been calls for the South Downs to be designated a national park.

The trail usually follows broad, clear, firm tracks over the gentle downs. You should be able to complete the walk within a week and it measures 102 miles (164km). There is a fairly good youth hostel and B & B provision, but only a few organised camp-sites. There are handy wayside water taps in places, if you're stuck for drinking water.

The South Downs Way starts with a choice of two routes from Eastbourne to Alfriston. It's possible to combine these, by walking from Alfriston to Eastbourne, then back to Alfriston to describe a long loop. If you choose this option, then the final distance would be around 114 miles (183km). Some walkers haven't yet accepted the extension to Winchester, preferring to end at the former terminus of Buriton. This is a pity, as Winchester is a fascinating little city and was once the King's Capital and a noted pilgrimage centre. There's also a place which has been handing out free beer for centuries, if you're interested!

Eastbourne to Alfriston (a)

12 miles (20km)

The footpath route leaves Eastbourne beyond the Martello tower known as the Wish Tower. A path climbs uphill from a signboard and crosses a scrub-covered downland. Simply follow the crowds on busy weekends to reach Beachy Head – an immense chalk cliff overlooking a 'stick-of-rock' lighthouse. Beware of the edge, which overhangs in places, though fractured parts have safety fencing. Walk downhill, then climb uphill past an old lighthouse at Belle Tout. A quick descent leads to food and drink at Birling Gap.

Ahead are the famous chalk cliffs known as the Seven Sisters. These are sheer cliffs separated by grassy combes. It's a fairly easy switchback route as you tick off each rise and fall to finish all too soon at Cliff End. Follow the Cuckmere River inland to Exceat Bridge. There is a camp-site and bunk-house nearby,

while a visitor centre deals with the local wildlife. Watch carefully for the route through woods to walk from Westdean to Litlington. Alfriston Youth Hostel lies across the Cuckmere River, but you could visit the village of Alfriston first.

Eastbourne to Alfriston (b)

12 miles (20km)

The <u>bridleway route</u> leaves Eastbourne to cross a different part of the scrub-covered downland. This line is closer to Eastbourne Youth Hostel, crossing a golf course and following a wooded escarpment overlooking Eastbourne. A descent leads towards the lovely village of Jevington. After climbing up a broad, wooded track, the South Downs Way crosses open downland and starts to descend above the head of the Long Man of Wilmington. You're looking at this famous giant hill-figure from completely the wrong angle. Try and fit in an evening visit to Wilmington for a better view of it. A good track leads down to the Cuckmere River and Alfriston. The buildings in Alfriston are charming and time should be spent exploring. The Clergy House was one of the National Trust's first acquisitions.

Alfriston to Pyecombe

22 miles (35km)

This is a long day's walk, but there are firm, clear tracks across gently rolling country so it shouldn't be too difficult. Hostellers could break the journey at Southease and walk off-route to Telscombe Youth Hostel. As the trail leaves Alfriston it climbs to the crest of the South Downs and offers views both seawards and inland across The Weald. Bostal Hill, Firle Beacon and Beddingham Hill are all part of this great crest, then the route descends to Itford Farm.

A bridge crosses the tidal River Ouse to reach Southease. A short road walk to Rodmell can be followed by a pub stop, or you can climb straight onto higher ground again. A good track crosses Swanborough Hill and overlooks Kingston near Lewes. After making a wide loop around the head of a valley, the trail descends to a busy road at the Newmarket Inn. You could break for food and drink before making a dash across the road. The route climbs into quieter country, but doesn't regain the true crest of the downs until it is near the scrub-covered Blackcap. Here, a broad track leads over some minor bumps, crosses a road at a car park which often features an ice-cream van, then climbs to 248m on the noted viewpoint of Ditchling Beacon.

The South Downs Way continues towards a popular pair of windmills known as Jack and Jill. Jill Mill is open most Sundays. They're both slightly off-route, but a visit is recommended. Head down to Pyecombe – a small village marooned between two busy roads. Accommodation is limited here, but Brighton has a fuller range of facilities, including a youth hostel, and it's only a short bus ride away.

Pyecombe to Amberley

21 miles (34km)

After leaving Pyecombe the trail takes us past a feature called the Devil's Dyke to reach the high crest of the downs again. An easy switchback leads over Fulking Hill, Perching Hill, Edburton Hill and Truleigh Hill in quick succession. Truleigh Hill has a youth hostel, but it's too early to stop. A descent leads to a busy road and there might be a snacks van parked in a layby. The nearby village of Botolphs has nothing to offer but views of its fine buildings. You'll notice the terminus of the Downs Link – a route joining the North and South Downs Ways using old railway trackbeds.

(*overleaf*) Walkers perched above the chalk cliffs of Beachy Head and its lighthouse

Walkers approach the wooded hill-fort of Chanctonbury Ring high on the downs

A gentle climb leads back onto the broad crest overlooking Steyning. Woodlands on the steep slope sometimes creep close to the track; while looking ahead you'll see a prominent clump of trees growing out of Chanctonbury Ring. On closer inspection you'll see that many trees on this ancient hill-fort have been damaged or toppled – victims of the hurricane of October 1987. The trail wanders downhill to cross a busy road, then heads for the heights again. A direct line leads over Barnsfarm Hill, Sullington Hill, Chantry Hill, Springhead Hill, Rackham Hill and Amberley Mount to descend to Amberley Station. Pubs and lodgings are available at Amberley and Houghton. Any spare time can be spent looking round an old quarry which has been transformed into a fine industrial museum.

Amberley to Buriton

22 miles (35km)

There are no facilities along this stretch of the South Downs Way, apart from a bunk-house at Gumber Farm. If you want anything, you'll have to walk off-route for it. This section of the trail is largely confined to forests and woodlands, and while it may trace the high crest of the downs there is little feeling of being in an upland area. Start the day by climbing from Houghton, then cross the back of Westburton Hill. Beyond Bignor Hill is a stretch of an old Roman road called Stane Street. This is equipped with a modern sign pointing to *Londinium* and *Noviomagus*. Look carefully for waymarks as there are several tracks and paths in the area. Note also the provision of a bunk-house at Gumber Farm.

A track descends from the downs at Littleton Farm, then heads straight back uphill for a long, forested walk over Graffham Down. Apart from odd clearings, there is no real break in the plantations until a wide gap is reached above the village of Cocking. Woodlands remain prominent on the next stretch, but the trail has been routed along an unplanted, cultivated swathe over Linch Down. These are the highest parts of the South Downs, reaching 250m.

There is a wooded area beyond Monkton House, then the route crosses a series of prominent little hills. Strangely, it wanders around the side of Beacon Hill, rather than going over it. Fairly simple walking ends the day, with broad tracks and minor roads being linked to reach Buriton. One part can be very muddy. Buriton was formerly the terminus of the South Downs Way and has a few B & Bs.

Buriton to Winchester

25 miles (40km)

After leaving Buriton, walkers and riders are sent along slightly different routes through the Queen Elizabeth Forest. Both lines converge on a visitor centre which offers refreshments. There's a climb onto Butser Hill, where a replica of an Iron Age farm has been built. The South Downs Way strives to keep high on Tegdown Hill, but there is little feeling of height. Although the route is far from the sea, it passes through a military base called HMS Mercury. A track leads over Wether

Down and descends to Combe Cross. The trail twists and turns as it crosses the slopes of Henwood Down, visits the fine buildings at Whitewool Farm, finally making its way towards the top of Old Winchester Hill.

The wrinkled frown worn by Old Winchester Hill is an ancient hill-fort. The area is also noted for its chalk downland flora. Keep an eye peeled for waymarks on the way through Exton. If you're struggling on such a long day's walk, then B & Bs can be found off-route in

Early morning mist fills the combes above the village of Houghton

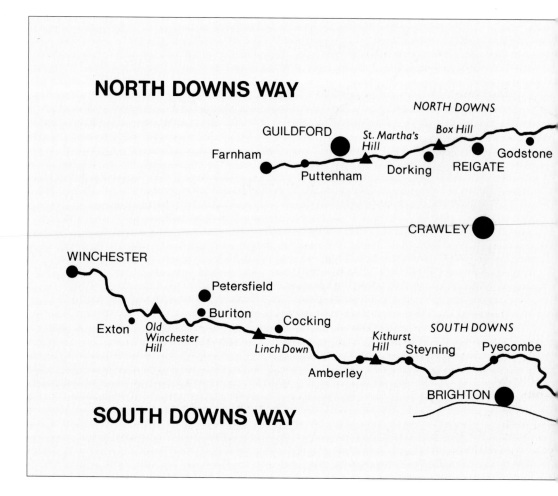

nearby villages. After crossing Beacon Hill and linking a series of farms you could enjoy a break at the isolated Millberrys Inn. After a road walk some fine, broad tracks are taken over Gander Down to Cheesefoot Head. There's a glimpse of Winchester in the distance, but you've still to get through the village of Chilcomb and cross a motorway before entering the city.

After the rural miles, Winchester seems a very busy place and has everything to satisfy the weary walker. It takes at least a day to visit all its interesting sites – the Cathedral, museums, Great Hall and King Arthur's Round Table. The youth hostel is in a splendid old mill in the heart of the city. You should also visit St Cross Hospital, knock on the door of the porter's lodge and ask for the 'Wayfarer's Dole'. You'll be handed a scrap of bread and a small beaker of ale – continuing a tradition of almsgiving which has spanned many centuries.

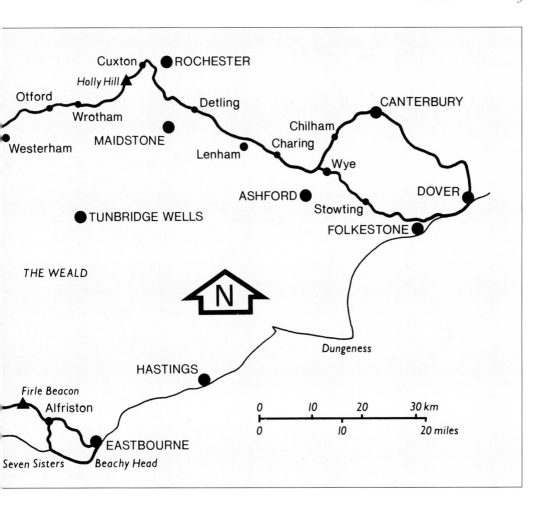

SOUTH DOWNS WAY INFORMATION

Schedule:

	miles	km
Eastbourne – Alfriston YH	12	20
Alfriston – Pyecombe for YH	22	35
Pyecombe – Amberley BB	21	34
Amberley – Buriton BB	22	35
Buriton – Winchester YH	25	40
Total distance	102	164

Maps:

OSGB 1:50,000 Landranger Sheets 185, 197, 198 & 199.

Guidebooks:

National Trail Guide, South Downs Way, by Paul Millmore, published by the Countryside Commission, Ordnance Survey and Aurum Press Ltd. *The South Downs Way & the Downs Link*, by Kev Reynolds, published by Cicerone Press. *The South Downs Way, Aerofilms Guide*, published by Ian Allen Ltd. *Along the South Downs Way to Winchester*, published by the Society of Sussex Downsmen. *A Guide to the South Downs Way*, by Miles Jebb, published by Constable & Co. Ltd.

Accommodation List:

The Society of Sussex Downsmen. South East England Tourist Board.

Path Association:

The Society of Sussex Downsmen.

Tourist Information Centres:

Eastbourne, Lewes, Brighton, Arundel, Petersfield, Winchester.

The North Downs Way (map pp.44-5)

The terms 'North Downs Way' and 'Pilgrim's Way' are often used interchangeably, but this is wrong. Originally, the idea was to designate the ancient Pilgrim's Way as a long-distance walking route, but as large stretches had gone under tarmac a number of alternative lines were suggested. The end product only occasionally coincided with the Pilgrim's Way, so the designated trail from Farnham to Dover was instead called the North Downs Way.

It's a fairly simple trail running through the wooded Surrey Hills Area of Outstanding Natural Beauty and the more open Kent Downs Area of Outstanding Natural Beauty. There are plenty of built-up areas, major roads and the awesome Channel Tunnel and its associated links. The North Downs Way does its best to steer a course past everything, but it also avoids several towns and villages, so you might have to make significant detours for food, drink and accommodation.

It's surprising that the route isn't more popular, as it's very handy for London and has excellent transport links with the city. Londoners could 'commute to walk' as easily as they commute to work. There are a few youth hostels along the way, but the gaps between them will need to be filled with lodgings at B & Bs. The North Downs Way isn't really a backpacker's trail as there are no real camp-sites and obtaining permission for a pitch could be difficult.

The distance is generally given as 141 miles (227km), but there is a choice of routes towards the end and the final distance could be as much as 150 miles (240km). Some walkers even complete both alternatives, ending with an enormous loop and pushing the total distance to almost 170 miles (275km). To keep things simple, the route is described from Farnham to Dover, ending with a choice of routes. If you want to 'do the loop' then you should allocate an extra two days. The main walk would take about a week to complete. The daily distances are high, but the walking is gentle and easy.

Farnham to Tanners Hatch

25 miles (40km)

Walkers arriving at Farnham by train will find a North Downs Way signpost before they reach the centre of town. Easy walking by riverside, road, fields and woods leads to the villages of Seale and Puttenham. The latter has a pub and shop. After crossing Puttenham Heath and passing some large farms on the line of the Pilgrim's Way, the trail passes close to Guildford. If you want to break this long day's walk into two easier days, then Guildford is the place to stay and the town is well worth exploring.

The North Downs Way climbs gently alongside a forest and follows a sandy track to the top of St Martha's Hill. The hill is crowned with a church which was raised from the ruins of a Norman chapel in 1840. When descending from the hill, look out for the Downs Link – a route joining the North and South Downs Ways using old railway trackbeds. Our way leads across an open slope to reach Newlands Corner – a popular place on the crest of the North Downs where snacks are usually available.

For the next leg, the trail is almost entirely confined to woodlands and forest. There are occasional clearings, as well as south facing viewpoints overlooking The Weald. The woodlands are interesting and all junctions of paths and tracks are marked, but keep an eye on your map and guide to be sure of your exact position. Blatchford Down is a fairly recent name for a patch of open downland. It was named in memory of Alan Blatchford, a founder member of the Long Distance Walkers' Association. The next open area is the crest of the downs at Ranmore Common. Just off-route and downhill is Tanners Hatch Youth Hostel.

Tanners Hatch to Godstone

21 miles (34km)

After passing Ranmore Church you'll find yourself above a vineyard, and it's not the only one along the North Downs Way. The River Mole can be crossed either by a bridge or stepping stones, depending on the rate of flow. A steep, stepped climb leads up the slopes of Box Hill – a well wooded escarpment devastated by the hurricane of October 1987. You'll be able to appreciate how much work went into reopening the trail by noting the number of sawn-off tree stumps. Food and drink are available on top of Box Hill by stepping off the path.

The North Downs Way clings to the escarpment, with only a few peeps possible through the trees. A huge chalk pit appears quite suddenly and waymarks show the safe way past it. The route wanders along the foot of the downs, then enters woods and zigzags back to the crest. Gentle walking along the crest on good tracks leads past a monument known as The Temple. A little further along is a large car park where food and drink can be obtained. Reigate is sprawled along the foot of the downs, if any greater needs have to be satisfied.

After heading through the extensive grounds of Gatton Hall School, the trail reaches Merstham, where there are shops, then crosses over and under a couple of motorways. A stretch of quiet country follows and the route enters woods to emerge near the village of Godstone. Limited B & B accommodation is available.

Godstone to Kemsing

20 miles (32km)

The day starts with another vineyard, then the North Downs Way climbs to a wooded crest. Trees toppled by the hurricane of October 1987 may now be regarded as a feature of the route. A railway tunnel has been bored beneath the downs and a sudden view aims straight along the line. Later, the trail runs close to a busy motorway. An ascent through woodlands near Titsey Park screens off a view of the motorway, then the path becomes rather narrow and overgrown. The highest parts of the North Downs are nearby, rising to 250m.

Woodlands seem to thin out as the trail leaves Surrey and enters Kent above Westerham. There are still plenty of trees, but these are often arranged in belts around large, cultivated fields. To negotiate this patchwork landscape, the North Downs Way has lots of corners built into its course, so that walkers don't tread all over 'The Garden of England'. A descent from the downs leads to the charming estate village of Chevening. Gentle tracks and paths keep to the low ground and the Pilgrim's Way leads through the lovely village of Otford. You could stay on the road to reach Kemsing Youth Hostel, or scale the ambitiously named Otford Mount and later take a signposted path to Kemsing from Hildenborough Hall.

Kemsing to Wouldham

21 miles (34km)

The route from Kemsing starts as a series of fiddly field paths, but suddenly becomes a more direct line when the Pilgrim's Way is joined. This leads along the edge of the village of Wrotham, then crosses a motorway. Later, the trail leaves the Pilgrim's Way and climbs onto the wooded crest of the North Downs near Vigo. There's a pub on the route before Trosley Country Park is entered. When the North Downs Way descends to pick up the

Kit's Coty is all that remains of an old burial chamber near Maidstone

line of the Pilgrim's Way, a slight detour can be made to include Coldrum Long Barrow. Another short section of the Pilgrim's Way ends with a sudden climb up Holly Hill, where woodland tracks can be very muddy.

After passing the village of Cuxton the North Downs Way crosses the Medway Bridge in the company of heavy traffic. It isn't known how the Pilgrim's Way crossed the tidal River Medway, but a number of fords could have been employed upstream. Rochester lies off-route – an interesting town with several points of antiquity. If nothing special is needed there, then stay on the trail for a while and seek B & B accommodation in the village of Wouldham.

Wouldham to Lenham

20 miles (32km)

After following a high-level track and road, the trail descends past the remains of a burial chamber called Kit's Coty. Not far off-route are the scattered blocks of Little Kit's Coty, also known as the Countless Stones. The route immediately heads back uphill to regain the crest of the downs. After taking a line between woods and fields for some distance, the trail passes the village of Detling, near Maidstone. Look carefully for waymarks and follow your map and guide closely to cross the downs above Thurnham. The way is easier to follow above Broad Street, then it descends to Hollingbourne and its pub.

A fine and direct length of the Pilgrim's Way comes next, but the journey must be broken at some point, perhaps at Lenham, where a little B & B accommodation can be found.

Lenham to Canterbury

25 miles (40km) See below.

Lenham to Stowting

21 miles (34km)

The walk along the Pilgrim's Way from Lenham is quite plain and obvious, cutting straight across cultivated country at the foot of the North Downs. One stretch, however, is remarkably overgrown, despite being classified as a 'byway open to all traffic'. Charing is an interesting village with many points of interest, if you can spare the time for a village trail. The Pilgrim's Way continues as a broad stripe across the country, but becomes rather vague through

Eastwell Park. Boughton Lees is the next village and beyond that is the parting of the ways.

The route to Canterbury heads for Boughton Aluph, then crosses farmland to trace woodland tracks to Chilham. A castle could distract you for some time in this charming village, but Canterbury is still a fair stride away. This part of the North Downs Way is dominated by orchards. Walk through orchards to reach Chartham Hatch, then more orchards to reach Harbledown, then aim straight for Canterbury Cathedral. Your footsteps should lead – as all good pilgrims before you – to the spot where Thomas à Becket was murdered. You could also make a mini-pilgrimage through the Can-terbury Tales Visitor Centre, with Chaucer as your guide. The city has a full range of services, including a youth hostel.

The route to Stowting is quieter. Walk from Boughton Lees to Wye, with only a few orchards to negotiate on the way to the crest of the downs. Easy walking along paths and tracks leads past the large hollow known as the Devil's Kneading Trough. Minor roads and broad tracks pass above Brabourne, then the route descends and a road is followed through Stowting. There's a pub and limited B & B accommodation is available.

Channel Tunnel works spread over the sea below chalk cliffs at Dover

Canterbury to Dover

20 miles (32km)

There are a couple of orchards on the way out of Canterbury then, beyond Patrixbourne and its fine church, the trail runs close to a busy road. There is no clear escarpment to follow on this route, which is mainly quiet, unremarkable, undulating country. The villages of Womenswold, Woolage and Shepherdswell are passed, and you could break for food and drink at the last one. Field paths lead past Waldershare House and a lonely chapel to reach Ashley. From there, a more direct line along an old Roman road leads to Dover. The town's history spans many turbulent centuries and one way of taking it all on board is to visit the White Cliffs Experience. There are a number of museums which are largely occupied with military matters.

Stowting to Dover

18 miles (29km)

The route from Stowting to Dover is fiddly in places, so pay close attention to your map and guide. The North Downs Way climbs to the crest of the downs, then descends near Postling. An isolated hill is climbed on the way to Etchinghill. All of a sudden the landscape at the foot of the downs is riven by road and rail routes – all traceable to two black holes at Castle Hill. This is the Channel Tunnel, where a corner of England will for ever be a foreign field.

Throughout the last part of the walk from Folkestone to Dover, the Channel Tunnel road and rail links blight the scene. The cliff walk above the wooded Warren isn't too bad and on a clear day you can see the distant coast of Calais. However, below the famous White Cliffs, where waves once danced, there is now an industrial site. The trail moves very close to the edge of Shakespeare Cliff on the final descent to Dover. The town is immensely interesting and you should spend some time

exploring it. You might also consider walking along the alternative route to reach Canterbury and return to Boughton Lees, thereby ending the walk with an enormous loop.

NORTH DOWNS WAY INFORMATION

Schedule:	*miles*	*km*
Farnham – Tanners Hatch YH	25	40
Tanners Hatch – Godstone BB	21	34
Godstone – Kemsing YH	20	32
Kemsing – Wouldham BB	21	34
Wouldham – Lenham BB	20	32
Lenham – Stowting BB	21	34
Stowting – Dover YH	18	29
Total distance	146	235
OR	*miles*	*km*
Lenham – Canterbury YH	25	40
Canterbury – Dover YH	20	32
Total distance	152	244

Maps:
OSGB 1:50,000 Landranger Sheets 178, 179, 186, 187, 188 & 189.

Guidebooks:
National Trail Guide, North Downs Way, by Neil Curtis, published by the Countryside Commission, Ordnance Survey and Aurum Press Ltd. *The North Downs Way – a User's Guide*, published by Kent County Council.

Accommodation List:
South East England Tourist Board.

Tourist Information Centres:
Farnham, Guildford, Sevenoaks, Rochester, Maidstone, Ashford, Canterbury, Folkestone, Dover.

The Thames Path

The Thames has been a navigable river for centuries, though anyone proceeding upstream from London in the past would have encountered more and more obstacles. Towards the end of the eighteenth century, when canal systems were being developed around the country, the Thames became tied into the network and the navigation was improved. The Thames Commissioners were appointed, obstructions were cleared from the river, locks and weirs were constructed and a tow-path was created.

It's the old tow-path which forms the basis of the Thames Path, the same tow-path that created problems with the ultimate designation of the route as a national trail. In the past, the tow-path was created haphazardly and switched from bank to bank. Sometimes the switch would take place at a bridge, but sometimes a ferry was needed to take horses and handlers across the river. As these ferries ceased operating, it became impossible to follow the tow-path without making enormous detours in some places. Recently, however, new stretches of path have been created and new bridges have been installed to link broken stretches. To make things even better, the Thames Path traces the river from sea to source, so that you can enjoy every aspect of the Thames.

It would take you at least a day to walk through London, or much longer if you wanted to take in all the sights and points of interest. An ongoing programme of works is gradually revamping the riverside in the city, introducing walkways, greenery and sculptures, as well as highlighting heritage features. Beyond the built up parts of London there are large towns and villages which impinge on the river, but there are also more open spaces, more trees and more natural riverbanks.

This is a very easy walk, usually on good, firm surfaces. It measures about 190 miles (305km) and would take up to a fortnight to complete. It all depends how much time you spend exploring the towns and villages along the river. There are usually abundant B & Bs and there are a handful of youth hostels. Backpacking might be considered, but you won't be able to find a pitch in London. Only a few organised sites are available on the middle reaches of the river. If you do get stuck anywhere, a fairly good transport system will get you to some other place. Shops, pubs and restaurants are usually available throughout each day. The whole navigable length of the Thames is covered by various ferry or cruise operators, so you could tackle the walk in its entirety, then use various means to cruise back to the Thames Barrier from Lechlade.

Thames Barrier to Putney

20 miles (32km)

The Thames Barrier is a striking construction which is intended to keep tidal surges off the streets of London. The shiny metallic hoods which cover the powerful engineering look unnervingly like a row of sinking ships. There's a visitor centre to explain how everything works, then you can follow a paved path upstream. New pathways are constantly being created alongside the Thames through London, but there are gaps where walkers come up against grim dereliction or industrial sites. Eventually, the whole riverside will boast a paved pathway with trees and shrubs, but it will take years to complete. A handy tip — wear trainers rather than boots for this part.

Things cheer up at Greenwich, where heritage features include the Trinity Hospitale, Royal Naval College, the *Cutty Sark* and the diminutive *Gipsy Moth*. There's a detour from the river to get through Deptford, then the route passes interesting lock entrances and goes through the imaginative Docklands development. Rotherhithe Youth Hostel is passed, where you might want to base yourself for a more thorough exploration of the city. There's a glimpse of Tower Bridge, then some fiddly little moves away from the river. All the familiar sights of London begin to appear around successive bends in the river, with plenty of places to break for food and drink.

How many places could you hope to visit? There's the Tower of London, Southwark Cathedral and St Paul's. By way of contrast there's the Hayes Galleria, National Theatre and Royal Festival Hall. You'll quickly lose count of all the bridges as you move onwards, noting Big Ben and the Houses of Parliament. Vauxhall Bridge has to be crossed, but you can return over Chelsea Bridge to walk through Battersea Park. There's another drift away from the river at Wandsworth, but after walking through Wandsworth Park the trail reaches Putney Bridge. There are lodgings nearby, or you could take a short tube journey towards Holland Park Youth Hostel.

Putney to Molesey

17 miles (27km)

The Thames tow-path starts at Putney and the scene changes considerably. The bustling city is left behind and the banks of the river are tree lined. Large towns lie close to the river and these are really suburbs of London. After making a great loop around Barnes there's a stretch of tow-path which sometimes floods and it can be messy. Beyond Kew the trail runs alongside the Botanic Gardens and later there's a view of Kew Observatory.

Richmond comes suddenly into view and it has an attractive riverside. If you can spare time for a town trail you'll find it most interesting. The tow-path continues past Ham House, then goes through a wooded area managed as a nature reserve. Grey squirrels hereabouts are remarkably tame. At Teddington Lock the tidal limit of the Thames is reached, so all the levels upstream are controlled by locks and weirs. The locks are always impeccably maintained and planted with flowers. You can rest on benches at each lock and watch the boats coming through, or look for 'Historic Flood Marks' fixed to walls. The last flood worth recording was in March 1947.

At Kingston upon Thames, cross a bridge and walk on the north bank of the river. A broad track leads around Hampton Court Park to Hampton Court itself. You can wander around the gardens, or visit certain parts of the palace which are open. If you think your navigation is good, then try the famous maze! Cross over a bridge to regain the south bank of the Thames at Molesey, where B & B accommodation can be found.

Molesey to Windsor

21 miles (34km)

After leaving Molesey the Thames Path passes Molesey Lock and Sunbury Lock before reaching Walton-on-Thames. Next, the river features a couple of loops which have been bypassed by the Desborough Cut. Go along the cut, which seems unnaturally straight. Cross the river by ferry at Shepperton and follow a minor road alongside the river. Later, a path leads through fields to Chertsey Bridge. Most of the route onwards to Staines uses a riverside road, but there is often a path just alongside.

After leaving Staines the trail leads to Runnymede and passes Magna Carta Island. You could break for refreshments and try and decipher copies of the 'Great Charter' that was signed by King John in 1215. As one commentary has it: 'That's why in England we can do as we like, so long as we do as we're told!' After Runnymede the tow-path is close to a road, but it moves back into quieter country beyond Old Windsor. Again, a loop of the Thames is bypassed and the trail follows a straight cut.

You're not allowed to walk through Windsor

Home Park, but have to cross Albert Bridge, walk to Datchet by road and later cross Victoria Bridge. The Thames is followed closely to Windsor, where the town is dominated by Windsor Castle and hordes of visitors. Cross over a bridge to reach Eton. Between them, Windsor and Eton could provide a whole day's distractions. There is a youth hostel which can be reached easily from the next road bridge upstream.

Windsor to Henley-on-Thames

24 miles (39km)

If you wanted to spend a morning exploring Windsor and Eton, you could walk to Maidenhead in the afternoon and continue to Henley the following day. The whole day's walk, though long, is quite easy. The north bank of the Thames is followed past Boveney Lock, the flowery Thames Field and Dorney Reach to get to Maidenhead. Cross Maidenhead Bridge and follow a road alongside the river until the tow-path starts again at Boulter's Lock. Later there's a detour away from the Thames which leads through the interesting village of Cookham.

After regaining the tow-path, continue to Bourne End Rail Bridge where a footbridge has been added to give access to the north bank of the river. The Thames Path runs between the river and a railway to reach Marlow. It's worth making a short detour to Marlow Lock, where there's a view of the church steeple across a wide reach of the river. There's no doubting that the towns and villages are becoming more scenic and the river is offering more lovely views.

The tow-path continues from Marlow to Temple Lock, crosses the river, then leads onto a small island at Hurley Lock. Beyond Hurley the riverside meadow is sometimes like a huge car park, though backpackers have a handy riverside site here. There's a detour uphill and away from the Thames near Culham Court, leading through the village of Aston to return to the tow-path via Mill End Lock. Follow the Thames past Temple Island and Remenham to reach Henley-on-Thames. The town is famous for its regatta and has a good range of facilities and lodgings.

Henley-on-Thames to Streatley

22 miles (35km)

Having crossed the Thames to reach Henley, the trail stays on the north bank to continue upstream. The route passes Lower Shiplake, Shiplake Lock and Shiplake. There's a wooded stretch along a very loopy length of the river, then the path continues to Sonning Bridge. Two bridges and many arches have to be crossed to reach the south bank of the river. Continuing past Sonning Lock, there's a broad and grassy area to be crossed on the way to Reading. The town seems rather grim at first, but soon brightens as the trail passes the two busy bridges which link Reading with Caversham.

You may imagine you're back in the country, but Reading's suburbs extend to Purley-on-Thames. Leave the riverside at an inn sign for a detour around Purley, then regain the tow-path at Mapledurham Lock. A simple riverside walk leads to Pangbourne, where the river has to be crossed to reach Whitchurch-on-Thames. For a change, there's a short, hilly walk a little away from the river. This goes past Combe Park and through woodlands damaged by the hurricane of October 1987, where winds were funnelled through the Goring Gap. When the path returns to the riverside there's only an easy stroll remaining to reach Goring and Streatley. A fine view from Goring Bridge takes in a scenic lock. There are shops and pubs in Goring, with a youth hostel at Streatley.

Marlow's Parish Church, as seen from Marlow Lock on the River Thames

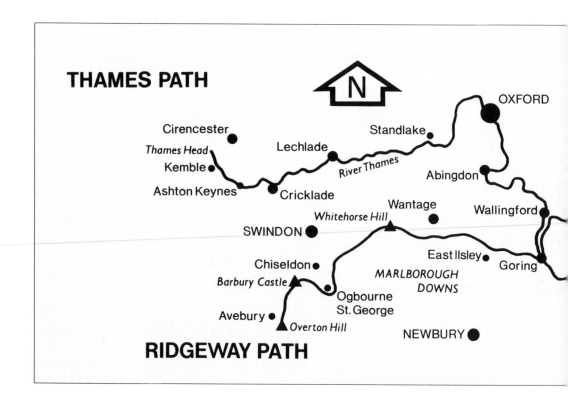

THAMES PATH

RIDGEWAY PATH

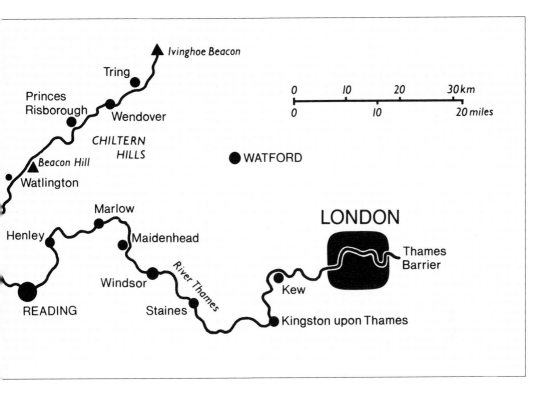

Streatley to Abingdon

21 miles (34km)

The Thames Path follows the river from Streatley to Wallingford, on the opposite bank to the Ridgeway Path. For the most part the path follows the riverside, but there is a stretch away from the banks by road through Moulsford. Wallingford is worth exploring, then the route continues to Benson Lock. Cross over the river to Benson, where backpackers have a site.

The trail continues to Shillingford, where you could study a comprehensive range of 'Historic Flood Marks' ending way above your head. There's a detour away from the river, but the tow-path is soon regained and leads onwards to Day's Lock. Cross the river at the lock and walk round a huge bend in the river to reach Clifton Hampden. At Clifton Lock the route goes through the Clifton Cut to avoid a bend in the river. After a long stretch punctu-

ated by a railway bridge, another bend in the river is bypassed at Culham Cut. The last part of the day's walk leads to Abingdon – a most interesting town with an attractive riverside and plenty of lodgings available.

Goring Bridge overlooks Goring Lock – a typical Thames lock

Abingdon to Newbridge

25 miles (40km)

This long day's walk assumes that you are simply going to follow the Thames. If you want to make a thorough exploration of Oxford, then you should spend the afternoon, night and even the next morning wandering around the city. There is an awful lot to take in, especially around the colleges, so you might want to spend a day or two there. There is a range of accommodation which includes a youth hostel and nearby camp-sites.

Walk upstream from Abingdon Bridge, changing to the south bank of the river at Abingdon Lock. The tow-path leads under a railway bridge and can seem remote from habitation for a while. Look carefully for the route at Sandford Lock, where you have to walk along an island between two channels of the river. The tow-path continues past Iffley Lock, but bypasses the centre of Oxford by way of Osney Lock. The trail crosses the river at one bridge, then comes back across the next.

Beyond Binsey is Godstow Lock and a busy road bridge.

The character of the Thames changes after Oxford. The navigation is less regimented and there are fiddly bends for boats to negotiate. The locks are now operated manually rather than mechanically. Walkers will find more gates and stiles along the tow-path. It's a pleasant walk from King's Lock to Eynsham Lock, passing a camp-site before reaching Pinkhill Lock. Technically, the tow-path continues to Bablock Hythe, then changes banks. Find out in advance if the ferry is running at Bablock Hythe. If not, then you'll have to cross the river at Pinkhill Lock and move away from the Thames before regaining its bank at Bablock. The stretch beyond the Ferry Inn at Bablock seems remote, passing Northmoor Lock and a solitary footbridge before reaching Newbridge. Accommodation is limited here to an inn and a small camp-site.

Newbridge to Lechlade

17 miles (27km)

The Thames starts to feature some wilder sections and the villages seem to be sited well away from the river. Facilities for walkers are limited to odd pub stops. Although the walk starts easily at Newbridge it soon runs into bushes and brambles. A large loop in the Thames is avoided by using an artificial cut at Shifford Lock, changing from the south to the north bank in the process. Tenfoot Bridge is a footbridge in the middle of nowhere, while Tadpole Bridge has a pub which offers B & B and a small camp-site.

A track leads from Tadpole Bridge to Rushey Lock, where you walk on the south bank of the river again. The Thames is becoming narrower and there are elaborate meanders

to trace on the way to Radcot Lock. The trail crosses two bridges to reach a pub at Radcot, then runs along the north bank of the river. There's an opportunity to visit the village of Kelmscott while on the north bank, then after crossing the river at Buscot Lock you could admire the lovely village of Buscot.

St John's Lock is the last lock on the river and there's a camp-site nearby. Pay homage to the statue of Old Father Thames – this once marked the source of the Thames, but was moved down to the navigable limit for safe keeping. An easy stroll across fields leads to Lechlade. There is a range of accommodation in this interesting little town.

Tenfoot Bridge and a Thames cruiser – note how narrow the river has become

Lechlade to Thames Head

24 miles (39km)

Owing to the absence of a tow-path upstream from Lechlade, field paths have been pressed into service to allow walkers to continue to the source of the Thames. These aren't always near the river, but in places new paths have been created to help maintain the theme. Walk from Lechlade to Inglesham, then continue along the river until routed away from it along a bridleway. Little is seen of the river until Castle Eaton, then it's followed more closely to Cricklade. The river dwindles significantly. If you want to break this long day's walk, then do so at Cricklade.

There's a good stretch of riverside path away from Cricklade, then tracks are followed around flooded gravel pits to reach Ashton Keynes. This area is now known as the Cotswold Water Park. Note how narrow the Thames has become – you might be able to jump across it. Follow it to Neigh Bridge Country Park near Somerford Keynes, then on to Ewen. In dry weather, the river bed may be empty. Beyond Ewen, cross a road near Kemble and head for a place where the Thames rises in wet weather. To reach the official source, however, you have to cross another road and walk across fields to reach a stone planted by the Thames Conservancy. There would need to be weeks of heavy rain before water would rise here, but this is the end of the walk. It seems like the middle of nowhere, but you can return to the road and head for the nearby Thames Head Inn. You'll be able to get a drink there, B & B if you need it, or a place to pitch a tent. Cirencester has a full range of facilities and can be reached by bus.

THAMES PATH INFORMATION

Schedule:

	miles	km
Thames Barrier – Putney for YH	20	32
Putney – Molesey BB	17	27
Molesey – Windsor YH	21	34
Windsor – Henley-on-Thames BB	24	39
Henley-on-Thames – Streatley YH	22	35
Streatley – Abingdon BB	21	34
Abingdon – Newbridge BB	25	40
Newbridge – Lechlade BB	17	27
Lechlade – Thames Head BB	24	39
Total distance	191	307

Maps:

OSGB 1:50,000 Landranger Sheets 163, 164, 174, 175, 176 & 177.

Guidebooks:

The Thames Walk, by David Sharp, published by the Ramblers' Association. *The Thames Path*, by Leigh Hatts, published by Cicerone Press. *A Guide to the Thames Path*, by Miles Jebb, published by Constable & Co. Ltd.

Tourist Information Centres:

London (several), Richmond, Kingston upon Thames, Walton-on-Thames, Windsor, Maidenhead, Henley-on-Thames, Reading, Wallingford, Abingdon, Oxford, Faringdon, Cirencester.

The Ridgeway Path

(map pp.56–7)

Some call it the oldest road in the world, while others have their doubts, but the Ridgeway has been trodden for more than 5,000 years. In the beginning was the Great Ridgeway – a coast to coast line from Dorset to East Anglia. It stayed on the high ground and afforded Bronze Age traders a good cross-country route. Over the centuries the Great Ridgeway has been cut apart by agriculture and incorporated into other routes. The last open stretches are found on the Wessex Downs passing the stone circles, hill-forts and burial mounds of our remote ancestors.

The remnants of the Great Ridgeway form the basis of the Ridgeway Path. It's useful to think of the path as two distinct stretches. The walk through the Wessex Downs Area of Outstanding Natural Beauty from Avebury to Streatley is almost entirely routed along the Great Ridgeway. The walk over the Chiltern Hills Area of Outstanding Natural Beauty from Streatley to Ivinghoe uses a variety of ancient and modern paths and tracks. Altogether, the route measures about 85 miles (137km).

There's a reasonable youth hostel provision for walkers, but B & Bs will have to be used to fill the gaps in the chain. Backpacking is possible, but there aren't really any organised sites, so you'd have to ask for permission in places. There seems to be no real objection to tents being pitched alongside the path over the Wessex Downs, as long as they don't block the way for farm vehicles. Note that in summer the ground sets like concrete, while in winter it can be sticky with mud. Water can be a problem, so taps have been sited at intervals over the Wessex Downs. Aim to take about a week over this trail and enjoy its ancient history.

Avebury to Ogbourne St George

12 miles (19km)

The official start of the Ridgeway Path is by the side of the road on Overton Hill. Anyone with a soul to be stirred, however, will start from Avebury after studying the immense stone circle which surrounds the village. This is a world heritage site and there are plenty of interpretative facilities if you want to learn all about the place. Follow the Stone Avenue away from the village, then walk via West Kennett to Overton Hill. Have a look at the site known as The Sanctuary before starting the walk. This pre-dates Avebury's circle and was linked to it by the Stone Avenue. The surrounding downs are scored and pock-marked with earthworks which we have no hope of understanding.

The route needs no detailed description as it sails over the downs and is quite free of stiles and gates. Look out for the Grey Wethers – lumps of rock which look like grazing sheep, some of which were dragged down to Avebury to build the stone circle. Barbury Castle is the first of a series of hill-forts – always located high on the downs and surrounded by circular banks and ditches. The Great Ridgeway descends to Chiseldon, but the Ridgeway Path stays high and follows Smeathe's Ridge before descending near Ogbourne St George. There is limited B & B accommodation here.

Ogbourne St George to the Ridgeway Centre

20 miles (32km)

Leaving Ogbourne St George, a series of tracks lead towards the hill-fort of Liddington Castle, which can be visited by crossing a field. The Great Ridgeway is encountered again at Foxhill, where the Shepherds Inn serves food and drink; last chance for some time. Nothing impedes the old road as it marches across the downs. Look out for Wayland's Smithy – an enormous stone-fronted burial chamber surrounded by trees.

Beyond Wayland's Smithy is the hill-fort of Uffington Castle, which is the highest point on the Ridgeway Path at 261m. Carved into the northern hill slope is a stylised white horse and some say that St George slew the dragon on the little hill below, the one with the white spot where the dragon's blood fell and no grass has ever been able to grow. The Ridgeway Path continues towards the next hill-fort, which is Segsbury Castle. At the next road, the Ridgeway Centre Youth Hostel lies just off-route. It's sited among a huddle of wooden buildings and saves having to walk down to Wantage for accommodation.

The Ridgeway Centre to Streatley

12 miles (19km)

After leaving the Ridgeway Centre a short walk leads to a monument to Baron Wantage. It is largely due to his influence that so many stately beeches were planted in copses and shelter belts on the downs. The surrounding land is more cultivated than on the previous day and the chalk escarpment is less well defined. Several wide tracks branch from the Ridgeway Path and there are a number of horse gallops which impinge on the route. Keep an eye on your map and guide to avoid being drawn along the wrong track.

A number of broad, gentle combes have been cut into the last part of the Wessex Downs and a track leads down one of these to reach Streatley and Goring. Goring Gap, where the River Thames cuts between the Wessex Downs and the Chiltern Hills, is the natural halfway point on the Ridgeway Path. There is a youth hostel at Streatley, while a number of shops and pubs can be found across the bridge in Goring.

Streatley to Watlington

15 miles (24km)

More towns and villages are visited on the second half of the Ridgeway Path, so it's easier to find food, drink and accommodation. Leave Goring by following the River Thames, towards Wallingford, on the opposite bank to the Thames Path. You'll notice the stiles and gates after the freedom of the Wessex Downs. A mysterious earthwork known as Grim's Ditch leads up into the Chiltern Hills. Keep an eye open for waymarks around Nuffield, as the trail crosses a golf course and a series of fields.

The Ridgeway Path makes use of the broad, clear course of the Icknield Way along the foot of the Chiltern Hills. The way can sometimes be very muddy. There should be no difficulty with finding the route, but keep your map and guide handy so that you'll know when to move a little off-route to Watlington. This interesting little town has shops, pubs and lodgings.

Watlington to Wendover

17 miles (27km)

The Icknield Way is followed away from Watlington, then it goes beneath a motorway. Beacon Hill is just beyond, managed as a nature reserve on account of its classic chalk grassland and varied flora. Hedges flanking the Icknield Way screen walkers from an unsightly gravel pit near Chinnor. The trail climbs up a wooded escarpment, then a roundabout series of field-paths eventually lead towards Princes Risborough. Tiny Lodge Hill is scaled before the route wanders around the edge of town.

The route to Wendover is fairly complex, but well marked. Field-paths and woodland walks lead steeply uphill, then a visit is made to Whiteleaf Cross carved on the hillside. There's a pub called The Plough on the way to Chequers – the country retreat of prime ministers. The house is given a wide berth and there may be shadowy figures hovering around to make sure you stay on the path. A monument stands on Coombe Hill where excellent views stretch northwards. The Ridgeway Path wanders through woodlands and across open spaces before descending to Wendover. There are shops, pubs and lodgings here, as well as a number of fine buildings.

Wendover to Ivinghoe

13 miles (21km)

A circuitous route leads from Wendover to Wendover Woods, which rise above the town. There are fine stands of beech on the Chilterns and although this is the highest part of the range there is little feeling of height. Paths, tracks and woodland walks lead towards Tring. A canal is crossed near Tring Station, but the route doesn't lead down to the town.

Grim's Ditch is encountered on Pitstone Hill and it tempts walkers downhill. The course of the Ridgeway Path, however, is along a different line. A scrubby woodland is passed on the way to Ivinghoe Beacon, where a simple walk uphill gains the summit. This is the official end of the walk and a fine viewpoint. For practical purposes, you'll have to descend to the road and head for Ivinghoe village. There's an interesting windmill to study and a nearby youth hostel.

RIDGEWAY PATH INFORMATION

Schedule:	*miles*	*km*
Avebury – Ogbourne St George BB	12	19
Ogbourne – the Ridgeway Centre YH	20	32
The Ridgeway Centre – Streatley YH	12	19
Streatley – Watlington BB	15	24
Watlington – Wendover BB	17	27
Wendover – Ivinghoe YH	13	21
Total distance	89	142

Maps:
OSGB 1:50,000 Landranger Sheets 165, 173, 174 & 175.

Guidebooks:
National Trail Guide, The Ridgeway, by Neil Curtis, published by the Countryside Commission, Ordnance Survey and Aurum Press Ltd. *The Ridgeway,* combined map/guide published by Footprint.

Path Association:
Friends of the Ridgeway.

Accommodation List;
Ridgeway Officer, Oxfordshire County Council.

Tourist Information Centres:
Avebury, Wallingford, Wendover.

The Peddars Way and Norfolk Coast Path

(map p.66)

The Peddars Way and Norfolk Coast Path sounds like two quite separate walks joined together – and indeed it is. The Peddars Way is a fine, long Roman road while the Norfolk Coast Path is a collection of paths and tracks linked to form a coastal route. It's been said that the Peddars Way starts in the middle of nowhere, ends in the middle of nowhere, and doesn't go anywhere in between. Maybe, but at least it's direct. The Romans probably constructed it in the first century, after Queen Boudicca's Iceni revolt. The old road crosses the remnants of the Breckland heaths, now largely under cultivation or forested. Shops, pubs and lodgings tend to be off-route, but Castle Acre is halfway and has everything you'll need.

The Norfolk Coast Path is often surprisingly distant from the sea due to extensive saltmarshes, sand dunes and mudflats. There are crumbling clay cliffs near Sheringham and Cromer. Sea defences occur as dykes or heaps of shingle, raised and strengthened after the disastrous tidal surge of 1953. Charming villages with their distinctive signboards provide plenty of distractions. There are churches, museums, shops,

pubs, ice-creams and pots of tea. Nature reserves are found and most of the coast has been designated both as an Area of Outstanding Natural Beauty and heritage coast.

This is an easy walk on good paths and tracks, measuring 93 miles (150km). It's mostly gentle, rolling countryside. There are two youth hostels and two other places where YHA members can get a discount on B & B rates. Backpacking could also be considered, as there are small, informal sites inland and large organised sites around the coast. Although each of the suggested day's walks are quite long, you could cut them in half and take about a week over the walk. Places with accommodation are noted.

Knettishall Heath to Castle Acre

25 miles (40km)

There is no real public transport to the start of the Peddars Way at Knettishall Heath, and no handy accommodation either. Backpackers who start late in the day can break at the Thorpe Woodlands camp-site, which has a small shop, not far into the trail. Walkers who have spent a night at nearby Thetford could get an early taxi to the start. Wooded paths lead

Walkers follow a long, straight stretch of the Peddars Way near Fring

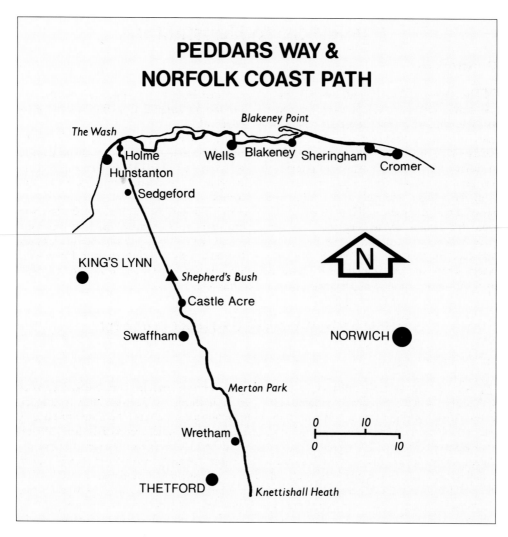

across the Little Ouse River. After passing through Thorpe Woodlands and crossing the River Thet, shelter belts of trees are followed to reach Brettenham Heath. This is one of the few remaining Breckland heaths and is managed as a national nature reserve. Good tracks lead through a quiet forest to reach the village of Wretham. Shops, pub and B & B accommodation are on offer, if you want to break this long day into two easier ones.

The Peddars Way continues through a forest to brush past the Stanford Practical Training Area. This is a military zone featuring live firing. Occasional manoeuvres can spill over the trail, but hopefully you'll be given due warning! In the midst of all this activity is Thompson Water, managed as a nature reserve. The original line

of the Roman road has been lost later, so paths, tracks and roads are used to zigzag through Merton Park, Little Cressingham, South Pickenham and North Pickenham.

The old straight track is found again where it bypasses Swaffham and is locally known as the Procession Way. Roads and tracks finally lead to Castle Acre. This pleasant village has grown around the ruins of a fortified Norman country house. There is also a sizeable priory whose dressed stonework contrasts with Norfolk's usual brick and flint architecture. The Old Red Lion was once a pub, but now provides hostel type accommodation. YHA members are offered a discount. There are shops and pubs in the village.

Castle Acre to Hunstanton

22 miles (35km)

The Peddars Way is under tarmac as it leaves Castle Acre, but there are some roadside paths which may be used. A gentle rise leads to 92m at Shepherd's Bush, then the Peddars Way cuts a broad stripe across country to distant Ringstead. Though hardly remote, this grassy or gravel track keeps its distance from the villages and only a few farms are passed. Food, drink and odd B & Bs are all off-route. It's a good idea to keep your map and guide handy as you march across this broad landscape, so that you can keep a check on exactly where you are. Sometimes the route is lined with bushes, but at other times it passes cultivated fields. If you wanted to break this day into shorter lengths, then find a B & B at Sedgeford.

Ringstead has a shop, pub and nearby bunk-house. The nearby seaside resort of Hunstanton has a youth hostel and a fuller range of services. Strangely, the Peddars Way doesn't join the Norfolk Coast Path end-on, but runs into it near Holme next the Sea. Technically, the coast path starts at Hunstanton and later runs past Holme, but it's up to you whether you walk to Hunstanton just to walk back again. Either way, the character of the walk changes considerably in this area.

Hunstanton to Wells-next-the-Sea

25 miles (40km)

A walk along a low chalk cliff at Hunstanton leads to a number of chalets in some sand dunes. After walking round a golf course the end of the Peddars Way is passed near Holme. A wooden walkway wanders through the Holme Dunes Nature Reserve, which has a profuse birdlife. The dune belt is replaced by a sea wall which passes saltmarshes to reach the village of Thornham. Almost every coastal village offers a shop, pub and some sort of accommodation.

The coast path has to take a fair step inland at Thornham, regaining the coastal theme at Brancaster, where a wooden walkway leads to Brancaster Staithes. In this area, a Roman with the title 'Count of the Saxon Shore' was required to repel continental raiders. In later centuries a young boy at Burnham Thorpe grew up to become Admiral Lord Nelson. Further away, at Burnham Deepdale, there's another bunk-house for walkers. There are half a dozen Burnhams clustered around Burnham Market and the trail leads from Burnham Deepdale to Burnham Overy Staithe along a sea wall. Look out for a prominent windmill.

Another sea wall leads towards extensive dunes at Holkham Bay. If the tide permits, you'll find easier walking along the broad, sandy beach. Come ashore again at Holkham Bay and walk through an area planted with pines, reminiscent of the forested Breckland. Eventually, a stout sea wall can be followed into Wells-next-the-Sea. This resort has everything you'll need, and the Old Exchange B & B offers YHA members a discount.

Wells-next-the-Sea to Cromer

25 miles (40km)

Follow the coast path away from the harbour at Wells, to pass extensive saltmarshes between Stiffkey and Cley next the Sea. The National Trust have an information centre at Morston which includes an observation room where you can gain a bit of height and look across to Blakeney Point. Boatmen run trips to the point from Morston and Blakeney, so that visitors can watch seals and spot a range of birds. After walking from Morston to Blakeney, a sea wall leads around the marshes to Cley next the Sea. There are rustling reed beds near the charming village and if you want to break your journey here you'll find that even the windmill offers B & B!

Extensive marshes and lagoons near Cley are protected by an immense bank of shingle. This is very difficult to walk upon, but there's little choice. On one side of the bank are booming waves, while on the landward side, somewhere in the reeds, you might hear a booming bittern. Bird watchers will probably always outnumber all other visitors as the area has an incredible range of species. A military installation near Weybourne, while being unattractive, is a feature to aim for as it marks the end of the long trudge on the shingle bank.

Easier walking leads towards Sheringham tracing a low line of crumbling clay cliffs. Beware of the edge, or of any suspicious cracks in the ground. A golf course and a steep little hill are crossed before Sheringham is reached. There is a youth hostel, if hostellers wish to drop out early. Alternatively, press on to complete the walk and return to Sheringham by bus or steam train. Cromer is reached by following a fiddly series of paths and tracks. The route is away from the sea and reaches the Roman Camp – at 102m the highest point in Norfolk. Cromer is worth exploring with a bird's-eye view of the town from atop the Parish Church tower.

PEDDARS WAY AND NORFOLK COAST PATH INFORMATION

Schedule:

	miles	km
Knettishall Heath – Castle Acre IH	25	40
Castle Acre – Hunstanton YH	22	35
Hunstanton – Wells-next-the-Sea BB	25	40
Wells-next-the-Sea – Cromer for YH	25	40
Total distance	97	155

Maps:
OSGB 1:50,000 Landranger Sheets 132, 133 & 144.

Guidebooks:
National Trail Guide, Peddars Way and Norfolk Coast Path, by Bruce Robinson, published by the Countryside Commission, Ordnance Survey and Aurum Press Ltd. *Peddars Way and Norfolk Coast Path*, published by the Peddars Way Association.

Accommodation List:
The Peddars Way Association.

Path Association:
The Peddars Way Association.

Tourist Information Centres:
Thetford, Watton, Swaffham, Hunstanton, Wells-next-the-Sea, Sheringham, Cromer.

The Wolds Way

(map p.72)

It's a curious thing, but the more the Wolds Way climbs, the more cultivated the surroundings become. The higher parts appear to be level plains divided into large fields, and it's only in the narrow, steep-sided dales that there's any sense of being in an upland area. This was formerly mixed farming country with small villages, but the populations were displaced to favour sheep rearing. In more recent years, the sheep have been displaced to favour intensive agriculture.

The Wolds Way follows a coast to coast route from the Humber estuary at Hessle to the battered rocky spine of Filey Brigg. The walking is fairly easy and measures 79 miles (127km). Given the amount of land under the plough, the trail has to zigzag around the corners of fields and walkers shouldn't be tempted to short cut across growing crops. The route often steers clear of what few villages there are in the Wolds, so you might be faced with detours in search of food, drink and accommodation.

Walkers on the Wolds Way will readily appreciate the meaning of Yorkshire's 'broad acres'. Some would be uninspired by the endless acres of grain, cereal or rape, while others would find the intensive crop production fascinating. It's all dry, chalky land and in summer it often needs spraying with water and nutrients. There's only one youth hostel, but there are a few handy B & Bs. It's also possible to backpack the route using small, informal camp-sites. Even novices should be able to complete the route within a week.

Hessle to Market Weighton

25 miles (40km)

There isn't a great deal of accommodation at Hessle, but good transport links help if you're staying somewhere nearby. Start on the shores of the Humber at the Ferryboat Inn and walk towards the graceful span of the Humber Bridge. This great feat of engineering is the world's longest single span and a nearby tourist information centre can supply details of its construction and specifications. The surrounding area has been developed as the Humber Bridge Country Park and includes a disused windmill.

The shore walk beyond the bridge is less scenic and a high tide could force you onto the streets of North Ferriby. A wooded walk leads inland and a busy road is best crossed using a nearby footbridge. After passing a large chalk pit the scene cheers up greatly. Welton is a charming village with several points of interest. The highwayman Dick Turpin was arrested at a pub called the Green Dragon. Old mills are passed on the way into the wooded Welton

The graceful span of the Humber Bridge features near the start of the Wolds Way

Dale. You'll quickly become attuned to Wolds agriculture – cereal crops, oilseed rape, a few sheep, cattle, and pigs to ensure that nothing goes to waste. Pheasants are reared for game in the woods. The villages of Brantingham and South Cave are a little off-route. South Cave has lodgings if you want to split this long day's walk into two easier stretches. There are also shops and pubs if you simply need food and drink.

A disused railway trackbed is followed into a wooded dale and East Dale leads towards high, open fields. The trail descends into Swindale and keeps away from the village of North Newbald. A broad green road climbs uphill and it continues as a tarmac road. There's a solitary farmhouse offering B & B and camping at Arras, but if you need a greater range of facilities, then go to Market Weighton. The town is reached by staying on the Wolds Way a little longer, then walking along a disused railway now known as the Hudson Way. The route is named after a man who made, and lost, a fortune on the line.

Market Weighton to Thixendale

21 miles (34km)

Walk back to the Wolds Way in the morning and follow the route through the village of Goodmanham. Cross a busy road to enter Londesborough Park. Artificial lakes have been created and are popular with wildfowl. A telescope has been mounted to allow you to view in detail. A road, track and path lead from Londesborough towards Nunburnholme. Try and obtain the key to the church here and have a look at a 1,000 year old stone cross. The trail stays high above the village of Millington and traces the high edge of Millington Dale. There are two steep-sided feeder dales which have to be crossed and as the slopes are too steep to be ploughed they support bushes and a range of grasses and flowers.

At the head of Millington Dale are level acres before a slight descent passes the village of Huggate. The Wolds Inn is popular with walkers who are prepared to make a short detour. A lovely grassy dale called Holmdale leads gently uphill to Fridaythorpe, where there are pubs and a small shop. Don't leave without visiting the little Norman church, which is easily missed. The Wolds Way crosses West Dale, then follows another dale, which leads into a network of small dales. This could explain the name of Thixendale, variously suggested to mean six dales or even sixteen dales. There are a youth hostel, shop, pub and tearoom in this pleasant setting.

Thixendale to Sherburn

20 miles (32km)

Throughout yesterday's walk, the Wolds gradually built up in height until they were just over 200m. On today's walk they reach the same level, then begin to diminish again. After climbing out of one dale and crossing another dale, the trail narrowly misses the deserted village of Wharram Percy. Walkers should feel obliged to make a thorough exploration of the site. It's one of the most famous deserted villages. It lost its population in the sixteenth century, partly because of the Black Death and partly through the increased use of land for sheep rearing. Helpful signs around the site explain things.

The Wolds Way leads through Wharram le Street, where you might get a pot of tea. There's nothing else on offer until the end of the day. The route crosses Settrington Beacon and runs close to the village of Wintringham. After climbing uphill through a small forest the trail is routed along the edge of the chalk escarpment and there are views towards the North York Moors. Sherburn is just off-route and it has a handy shop, pub and lodgings.

Wolds-style agriculture, colour and scenery at Londesborough Park

Sherburn to Filey

17 miles (28km)

The last day's walk is fairly gentle, as the Wolds peter out towards the North Sea. A low-level series of paths and tracks lead to Ganton, where a climb leads past a sensitive military installation on Staxton Wold. Hurry past the barbed wire and forbidding notices. The Wolds Way leads across a couple of dales, then follows a couple more. Good tracks finally lead down to Muston. There's a pub on the route in the village, but it's not far to Filey now and seaward views already include Flamborough Head and Scarborough Castle.

You won't see Filey Brigg until you've found your way through the busy little resort of Filey. Follow signposts for the Coble Landing, where fishing boats are brought up alongside an amusement arcade. The Wolds Way traces a low, crumbling clay cliff towards Filey Brigg, but if the tides allow, you could walk along the beach. The Brigg is best visited at low water as a long, rocky reef is exposed. Some say it is the bony remains of a dragon. You can inspect rock pools, but beware of slippery seaweed and freak waves. The Wolds Way meets the Cleveland Way a little further along the coast at a lonely stile. This is bureaucratic nonsense – both routes should terminate at Filey. You could, of course, continue straight into the Cleveland Way for a longer walk.

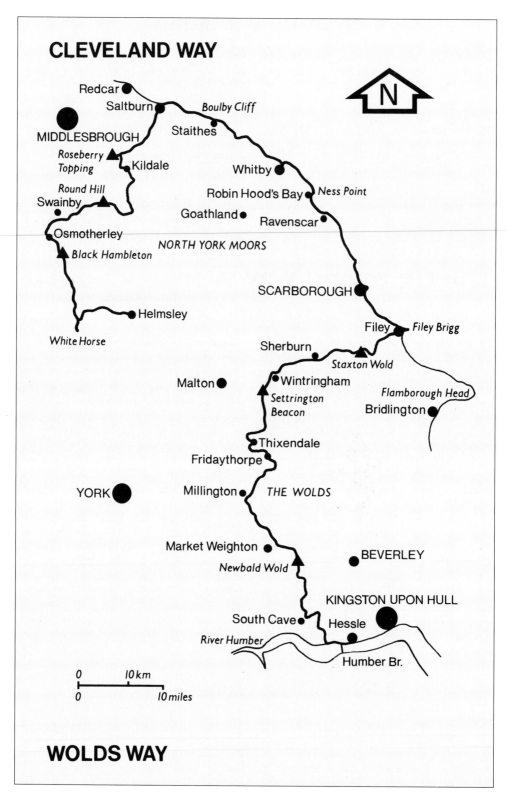

WOLDS WAY INFORMATION

Schedule:

	miles	*km*
Hessle – Market Weighton BB	25	40
Market Weighton – Thixendale YH	21	34
Thixendale – Sherburn BB	20	32
Sherburn – Filey BB	17	28
Total distance	83	134

Maps:
OSGB 1:50,000 Landranger Sheets 100, 101, 106 & 107.

Guidebooks:
National Trail Guide, Wolds Way, by Roger Ratcliffe, published by the Countryside Commission, Ordnance Survey and Aurum Press Ltd. *The Wolds Way*, by David Rubinstein, published by Dalesman Publishing Co Ltd.

Accommodation List:
Humberside County Council.

Tourist Information Centres:
Humber Bridge, Beverley, Filey.

The Cleveland Way

(map p.72)

The Cleveland Way comes in two parts, an inland moorland stretch and a coastal cliff path, making the 108 miles (174km) circuit from Helmsley to Filey a walk of great contrasts. Most of the route lies within the North York Moors National Park, while the seaward length is also designated heritage coast. In the early years of the Cleveland Way the paths were largely overgrown. Increased usage led to serious erosion in many places and repair work is still continuing. This has left the Cleveland Way with some good, firm dry surfaces and many steep slopes now feature steps. You should have little trouble with route finding and should be able to cover the distance speedily and easily.

The route can be completed in a week, but give some thought to your accommodation before striding across the moors. There are many empty stretches where it's difficult to find food, drink and lodgings. The coastal stretch, however, has a number of small towns and villages and there's an excellent range of shops, pubs, restaurants and lodgings. Backpacking can be heartily recommended – there are small, informal sites not far from the moors and plenty of organised sites along the coast. There are only a few youth hostels, but the gaps between them can be filled with recourse to B & B accommodation. A couple of bunk-houses are also available.

Cleveland derives its name from the cliff edges which surround the area, both on the seaward side as well as overlooking the Vale of York and Guisborough. The plateau-like nature of the North York Moors means that it will catch all sorts of weather. You'll bake in the summer heat and find no shelter from winter winds, rain or driving snow. Care is needed on the coastal cliffs in windy weather. The coast is also subjected to occasional morning mists, which can be annoying when both the inland moors and open sea remain clear.

Helmsley to Osmotherley

23 miles (37km)

Helmsley takes some time to explore properly, so it's handy if you can spend your first night there. It has a youth hostel, some B & Bs, but no camp-site. The first part of the Cleveland Way is a gentle stroll, missing Rievaulx and its fine abbey, heading through Nettle Dale,

The aggressive Wainstones seem out of character with the gentle moors nearby

Flassen Dale and the village of Cold Kirby. There's a pub and camp-site at Hambleton, before reaching the cliff line which overlooks the Vale of York. There's a detour along the cliff top to inspect the Kilburn White Horse, but you won't be able to see this great hill-carving properly from above. Retrace steps to Sutton Bank, where there is a visitor centre, informative displays on the area, and refreshments.

Continue walking along the cliff line, overlooking the wooded hollow enclosing Gormire Lake – the only natural lake in the area. The cliffs gradually become less steep and rocky, dwindling to become rugged, wooded slopes. High Paradise Farm is the last building for a while and offers B & B, a simple pitch for tents and snacks for passing wayfarers. Think twice before going on because there's nothing else on offer until Osmotherley.

There's a change of theme at this point, as the trail leaves the steep scarp slope and follows the Hambleton Drove Road across the heathery moors. This ancient route cuts straight across the high moors and was once so busy with drovers that an inn was built alongside. It's

your way. A series of hills are crossed which feature patches of moorland and small forests. One hill has a glider club on top and a quarried, eroded face. Look out for the Lord Stones Cafe, which is partly buried underground. There may not be another chance to buy a snack during the day's walk.

The Cleveland Way continues on a switchback course, following a reconstructed path up Cringle Moor. The descent from the far side is followed by another uphill, another downhill, then a steep and rocky climb past the celebrated Wainstones. These sharp angular blocks seem quite out of character with the moors, but are aggressively attractive. After crossing Hasty Bank and going down a steep slope, there might be a snacks van parked in a nearby car park, but don't rely on it. The next ascent leads close to the 454m summit of Round Hill, which is the highest point on the North York Moors. Note the Hand Stone and Face Stone, two ancient moorland waymarks, nearby.

Leaving Round Hill, note that the Coast to Coast Walk and Lyke Wake Walk run eastwards, while the Cleveland Way heads north. Follow the trackbed of an old ironstone railway across Ingleby Moor. If you're short of a few pence, then have a look on top of a stone pillar on the moor, where money is sometimes left for needy travellers. A long descent finally leads to Kildale, where facilities are limited to a shop, camping barn and a couple of B & Bs. If you're stuck for a place to stay, then a train ride could get you to some other place. A timetable and accommodation list would be handy, as you wouldn't want to miss a train or end up somewhere with even more limited choice.

gone now, so press onwards, passing close to the 399m summit of Black Hambleton before descending steps into Oak Dale. Osmotherley has a splendid range of services for a small village.

Osmotherley to Kildale

22 miles (35km)

After leaving Osmotherley the Cleveland Way is accompanied by unofficial routes such as the Coast to Coast Walk and Lyke Wake Walk, so don't assume that everyone is going

The delightful fishing harbour of Staithes and
its moored cobles

Kildale to Saltburn

16 miles (26km)

There's a forested stretch beyond Kildale,
then a climb to Captain Cook's Monument on Easby Moor. You could drop down to
Great Ayton to find out more about Captain
Cook, but you'll be visiting his maritime haunts
later at Staithes and Whitby. The unmistakable
profile of Roseberry Topping has been in view
since Osmotherley and the Cleveland Way
makes a detour to include its summit. Be
warned – the way is steep and badly eroded, but
the views across the plains are excellent.

Moorland paths and forest tracks lead from
Roseberry Topping to skirt Guisborough and
its priory. The town has a full range of services,
if you need anything. The first pub since
Osmotherley is reached at Slapewath and there's
a fish and chip shop on the trail at Skelton
Green. Saltburn is reached by following the
route through a wooded dale spanned by a lofty
railway viaduct. This genteel, planned Victorian
seaside resort has plenty of lodgings. If the road
down to the pier seems too steep, then use the
world's oldest cliff railway to descend.

Saltburn to Whitby

21 miles (34km)

While climbing Hunt Cliff above Saltburn
you can look back inland as far as
Roseberry Topping, but the moors have now
been forsaken in favour of the coast. An
industrial railway leads round the cliff to
Skinningrove, offset by strange iron sculptures.
A small museum at Skinningrove explains all
about the ironstone industry. Boulby Cliff is a
huge, rugged slope rising 200m above the sea.
It was once worked by alum miners and a row
of old mine cottages is reached later. One of
these is the Walkers Halt which provides snacks
and a free foot-care service for passing
wayfarers.

Staithes is a charming, compact fishing
village. If you want to stay there, accommodation ranges from B & Bs to an independent
hostel. Squeeze through the narrow streets and
search out Captain Cook associations. By way
of a complete contrast, the trail later passes the
derelict ironstone harbour of Port Mulgrave.
Runswick Bay is an attractive, steeply pitched
village where the Cleveland Way is forced along
the beach for a short way.

Kettleness isn't really a village these days, as
most of it fell into the sea one stormy night.
Sandsend is a small resort which heralds the
arrival of Whitby. It takes a while to fully
explore Whitby, a former whaling centre with
many nooks and crannies and a colourful

history. There's a youth hostel next to Whitby Abbey, reached by way of a steep, cobbled road or a whole pile of stone steps. The earliest lines of English literature were penned at the abbey and the movable date of Easter was agreed by the Synod of Whitby. Captain Cook sailed from the town and Bram Stoker chose to bring Dracula to the attention of the world via Whitby.

Whitby to Scalby Mills

21 miles (34km)

The walk from Whitby to Robin Hood's Bay is fairly easy, staying high on the crumbling shale cliffs above Saltwick Bay to reach Robin Hood's Bay. Part of the village was washed away in a storm, so a massive buttress holds the rest in place. A trip down the steep, narrow main street is recommended, but you'll have to retrace your steps to continue. The Coast to Coast Walk ends here.

A short walk leads to a steep-sided valley where Boggle Hole Youth Hostel can be found. The Cleveland Way tends to drift away from the sea as it climbs a rugged slope to reach Ravenscar. This was planned to be a major seaside resort, but very little was actually built. However, enough has been done to feed and accommodate passing wayfarers. The Lyke Wake Walk ends here. The cliff path from Ravenscar is narrower than the ones used so far, but the way ahead is fairly easy. Rugged slopes falling seawards are clothed in lush vegetation and appear quite wild. Hayburn Wyke is a secret little bay reached by descending a flight of wooden steps. Beyond Cloughton Wyke the cliff line is noticeably lower, but made of great slabs of rock, rather than crumbling shales. Gentle walking leads to Scalby Mills on the outskirts of Scarborough, where a short detour inland leads to a youth hostel and campsite.

Scalby Mills to Filey

12 miles (19km)

Scarborough has many features of interest and you should aim to spend the morning searching them out. Visit the cliff top castle and old church. You could use cliff lifts to commute between the main shopping street and the promenade. After passing a huge hotel you'll reach the spa which started making Scarborough a noted resort as long ago as 1626.

Some walkers dislike the final stretch of the Cleveland Way and even end their walk at Scarborough. They claim that caravan sites intrude too much on the trail, but things aren't that bad and the cliff scenery remains impressive. It's the end of the Cleveland Way which is rather silly – it terminates suddenly at a stile between two fields where the old North and East Ridings of Yorkshire once met. If you walk towards Filey Brigg for a thrilling finale, then you're actually following the Wolds Way. Maybe you'll want to continue towards the Humber.

CLEVELAND WAY INFORMATION

Schedule:

	miles	*km*
Helmsley – Osmotherley YH	23	37
Osmotherley – Kildale BB	22	35
Kildale – Saltburn BB	16	26
Saltburn – Whitby YH	21	34
Whitby – Scalby Mills YH	21	34
Scalby Mills – Filey BB	12	19
Total distance	115	185

Maps:
OSGB 1:50,000 Landranger Sheets 93, 94, 99, 100 & 101.

Guidebooks:
National Trail Guide, Cleveland Way, by Ian Sampson, published by the Countryside Commission, Ordnance Survey and Aurum Press Ltd. *Cleveland Way Companion*, by Paul Hannon, published by Hillside Publications. *Walking the Cleveland Way & Missing Link*, by Malcolm Boyes, published by Cicerone Press. *A Guide to the Cleveland Way*, by Richard Sale, published by Constable & Co Ltd. *The Cleveland Way*, by John Merrill, published by JNM Publications. *The Cleveland Way*, by Bill Cowley, published by Dalesman Publishing Co Ltd. *The Cleveland Way*, combined map/guide published by Footprint.

Accommodation List:
Cleveland Way Project Officer, North York Moors National Park Authority.

Tourist Information Centres:
Helmsley, Sutton Bank, Guisborough, Saltburn, Staithes, Whitby, Ravenscar, Scarborough, Filey.

The Pennine Way

The Pennine Way was the first long-distance walking route to be designated. It runs from Derbyshire to the Scottish borders and takes in plenty of broad, boggy moorlands as it wanders along the length of the Pennines and Cheviot Hills. It's the first choice for many newcomers to long-distance walking, but the failure rate is high and many of these hopefuls would have been better advised to start with an easier trail. You'll find this is a tough walk and there are parts which can seem remote from habitation.

It's probably going to take most walkers between two and three weeks to complete the Pennine Way and the distance is variously quoted as between 250 miles (400km) and 270 miles (435km). The route crosses the Peak District, Yorkshire Dales and Northumberland National Parks, as well as the North Pennines Area of Outstanding Natural Beauty and the area generally known as the South Pennines. Maybe there's too much hype associated with the Pennine Way. It's been well walked and in places it's become severely eroded. A programme of repair works is currently in place, so the worst parts of the route should ultimately boast a good, firm, clear, weatherproof surface.

Despite having some remote stretches, the Pennine Way also has areas with abundant facilities and accommodation. Youth hostels, B & Bs and camp-sites are available at fairly regular intervals. There's a central booking service operated by the YHA, which allows wayfarers to book all their overnights in one go. Backpacking is highly recommended and anyone who doesn't want to carry a huge load can avail themselves of a service which will transport all their gear to their next overnight stop. Food, drink and farmhouse teas are on offer almost every day. There's also the camaraderie of the route – so you'll feel part of a greater scheme of madness! When you're comparing notes with other wayfarers, you'll come to realise that the worst parts of the route are always just ahead.

As the Pennine Way is an upland route frequently crossing bleak moorlands above 500m, you'll find that bad weather and poor visibility make it a potentially hazardous route. It's probably a good idea to have a couple of days in reserve in case of any mishap.

Edale to Crowden

17 miles (27km)

The Pennine Way used to leave Edale in two directions to scale Kinder Scout, the highest part of the Peak District. Walkers are now encouraged to start by ascending Jacob's Ladder, which is a firm and clear route. The original main route over Kinder Scout is a badly over-trodden peat bog. From the top of Jacob's Ladder, a firm path can be followed along a gritstone edge to reach a waterfall at Kinder Downfall. Parts of the trail run above 625m in altitude. Although it sounds quite wrong, Pennine wayfarers start in the deep end.

They say that most walkers who give up the Pennine Way do so during the first day. By the time you've crossed a boggy moorland and reached the Snake Road you may understand why. You may even want to exercise that option yourself. A new path and the line of Devil's Dyke leads to the broad, peaty summit of Bleaklow Head at 628m. The bare peat is becoming the hallmark of the Pennine Way and in wet weather it can make life miserable. A long descent keeps above Torside Clough to reach Torside Reservoir in Longdendale. This is far enough for the first day. A youth hostel and camp-site are close at hand at Crowden, and there's a chance to buy a few supplies too. Anyone continuing over Black Hill would need to be very sure of themselves, but a few folk do press on beyond Crowden on their first day.

Crowden to Standedge

13 miles (21km)

Leave Crowden and climb high above Laddow Rocks. The scene is bleak and ahead lies the bare, bald Black Hill. This is desperately boggy in wet weather. It used to be much worse, but legions of walkers are actually wearing away the peat to expose a firm surface in some places. The 582m summit is known as Soldier's Lump. There used to be two routes leaving Black Hill, but walkers are now advised to use the path and track leading down to the Wessenden reservoirs. This is reasonably firm, while the other route crossing Wessenden Head Moor, Black Moss and White Moss is appallingly boggy. You could walk all the way down to Marsden in search of shops, pubs and a range of accommodation, all off-route.

After passing Wessenden Lodge, the Pennine Way climbs back onto the higher moors

and reaches Black Moss Reservoir. The trail leads towards the main Standedge road, which runs through a cutting. There's a pub nearby, if you're in immediate need of refreshment. If you follow the road in the Oldham direction, you'll find Globe Farm. This place offers a camp-site, bunk-house, B & B accommodation and basic food supplies. It's not often you'll find such a wide range of facilities under one roof.

Youngate Bridge at the bottom of Jacob's Ladder (*Graham Thompson/Trail Walker*)

Standedge to Mankinholes

13 miles (21km)

An easy walk along the gritstone outcrop of Standedge is followed by a long stretch over broad, undulating moorlands. There's a road to cross, then later a footbridge spans a motorway which slices through the crest of the Pennines. The trail has been resurfaced on the way to the 472m summit of Blackstone Edge. As you descend from this rocky summit you'll find a remarkable, broad, cobbled road with a central gutter. A raging debate centres on whether this is a Roman road or a more recent route. The Pennine Way leaves it to cross the next road near the White House pub.

A series of high-level reservoirs are passed on good, firm tracks. Blackstone Edge Reservoir, Light Hazzles Reservoir and Warland Reservoir are passed in turn and an artificial drain feeding them is followed across the moors. Stoodley Pike, an enormous stone monument, has been in view for some time, but hostellers and backpackers go down to Mankinholes before reaching it.

Mankinholes to Ponden Hall

15 miles (24km)

After climbing to Stoodley Pike, a descent takes the trail past farms and through woodlands to cross the industrial Calderdale. If you need to do any shopping, you'll have to detour into nearby Hebden Bridge. A fiddly series of paths and tracks lead uphill again, passing Colden to cross Heptonstall Moor. After crossing Grainings Water you might consider a short detour to the Pack Horse Inn. The Pennine Way is routed along a reservoir access road passing the Walshaw Dean Reservoirs. A path leading up a broad moorland slope has been repaired in places, then after crossing Withins Height at nearly 450m a ruined farmstead is reached.

Top Withins has been held to be Emily

Brontë's *Wuthering Heights* and despite a dis-claimer fixed to the wall by the Brontë Society, hordes of literary pilgrims trek up to see the place. There's even a waymarked Brontë Way, which you'll follow on the way down to Ponden Hall. Hostellers might consider a long trek off-route to Haworth, but Ponden Hall offers a camp-site, B & B and snacks for passing wayfarers. It's also been identified as 'Thrushcross Grange' from *Wuthering Heights*.

Ponden Hall to Gargrave

17 miles (27km)

After leaving Ponden Hall the trail climbs gradually over Ickornshaw Moor, reaching 440m and revealing a view ahead of low, rolling fields backed by the distant Yorkshire Dales. The descent leads to a road and a slight detour can include the shops at Cowling. Fiddly field-paths, tracks and minor roads are followed for the rest of the day. Lothersdale is a pleasant village in a hidden dale, with a shop and pub. An easy climb to the 388m summit of Pinhaw Beacon reveals enough heathery moorland to remind walkers of the distant moors.

There is a youth hostel off-route at Earby, but most wayfarers would be able to cope with the trail as far as Gargrave. A break can be taken at a pub at Thornton-in-Craven, then an easy tow-path walk runs along the Leeds & Liverpool Canal. This takes the trail through East Marton and although the canal continues to Gargrave, you're routed through fields to get there instead. There are a camp-site, a few B & Bs, pubs and shops.

Gargrave to Horton-in-Ribblesdale

21 miles (34km)

This is a long day's walk, but you can break the journey by walking to Malham in the morning and spending the rest of the day exploring its surroundings. The following day,

you would continue to Horton. The walk to Malham is very easy and is a gentle introduction to the Yorkshire Dales. Field-paths are followed fairly close to the River Aire, passing the villages of Airton and Hanlith to reach Malham. The attractions at Malham include large scale features such as the great cliff of Malham Cove and the awesome chasm of Gordale Scar. There is a youth hostel, camp-sites, shop and pubs if you want to break here.

To continue to Horton, climb up alongside

Ascending Jacob's Ladder near the start of the Pennine Way (*Graham Thompson/Trail Walker*)

Malham Cove and cross the limestone pavement on top. Knobbly country is crossed to reach Malham Tarn, where a short woodland walk is followed by a stroll through a small valley. At the farmstead of Tennant Gill a path climbs up the slopes of Fountains Fell, passing its colliery-scarred 668m summit. Ahead lies Pen-y-Ghent, which the trail reaches by a circuitous route. The 694m summit is gained after scrambling up a couple of rock steps. Before reaching Horton, you'll be aware of the tremendous amount of remedial work which has been accomplished on surrounding paths. A walled track leads down to Horton, where there are a camp-site, bunk-house and B & Bs. Apart from the pub, you could also visit the celebrated Pen-y-Ghent Cafe and sign their Pennine Way Visitor Book.

The Roman road called Cam High Road is followed through the Yorkshire Dales

Horton-in-Ribblesdale to Hawes

15 miles (24km)

A series of excellent packhorse ways connect Horton and Hawes, so route finding is fairly easy even if the area being crossed seems rather remote. A long, walled track leads away from Horton, passing several gaping potholes as it crosses limestone country. The trail leaves this track and picks up another track at Old Ing. A stone bridge spans the chasm of Ling Gill, then a climb uphill leads onto an old Roman road at Cam End. While you're following this old road, note the remote farmstead of Cam Houses, which has a bunk-house and usually offers snacks for wayfarers.

Leave the Roman road at Kidhow Gate, where it is now under tarmac. A track skirts Dodd Fell at almost 600m, then starts to descend. A path cuts across Ten End to take the Pennine Way through the little village of Gayle on the way to Hawes. This little town has a full range of facilities and is well worth exploring. It's also the last good stocking-up point before Teesdale.

The Pennine Way leads across lightly snowed fields to reach Hawes in Wensleydale

Hawes to Keld

13 miles (21km)

An easy stroll leads from Hawes to Hardraw, where you have the option of paying a few pence to see the 30m plunge of Hardraw Force. A walled track nearby marks the start of the day's climbing, then the open slopes of Great Shunner Fell are gained. This is a gentle ascent, but it seems endless and it is over-trodden in places. Eventually, the 716m summit is reached and it proves to be a noble viewpoint. In mist, however, you'd have to be careful to leave in the right direction, as there are broad, sprawling moorlands in all directions. The descent finally leads to the little village of Thwaite in Swaledale. You might be able to get a snack before continuing to Keld.

A lovely limestone terrace is followed around Kisdon Hill and you should go down to the river and see the splendid waterfalls. Facilities at Keld are quite limited, but you'll find a youth hostel, camp-site and B & B. You'd need lots of spare time and energy if you wanted to continue, as there are bleak and empty moorlands ahead. The Pennine Way crosses the unofficial Coast to Coast Walk at Keld.

Keld to Baldersdale

15 miles (24km)

Walkers leave Keld and strain for a glimpse of the legendary Tan Hill Inn, the highest pub in England at nearly 530m. The trouble is, if you set off too early it won't be open, and if you set off later and spend any length of time there, you might not be able to complete the day's walk. It's something to consider as you plod across the moors. A dull stretch of moorland is crossed beyond Tan Hill Inn and the trail follows Frumming Beck downstream. Next, there's a choice of routes to consider.

The main route crosses the River Greta via the natural rock formation called God's Bridge.

After going over a busy road the trail crosses Bowes Moor, Deepdale Beck and Cotherstone Moor. A final descent leads into Baldersdale and runs close to the youth hostel beneath a huge reservoir dam. The alternative route follows the River Greta to Bowes, where there are a shop and pub. It's longer than the main route and later involves fording Deepdale Beck and following a minor switchback of moorland humps and bumps. After passing the gritstone cap of Goldsborough the route goes down into Baldersdale, passing close to the youth hostel. This is generally reckoned to be the halfway point on the Pennine Way.

Baldersdale to Langdon Beck

15 miles (24km)

Reservoirs dominate the morning's walk. After leaving those in Baldersdale and crossing enclosed moorland, more are found in Lunedale. Keep an eye on your map and guide as the trail leads from Lunedale over to Teesdale, as the route is fiddly in places. If you need anything special, you should be able to obtain it at Middleton-in-Teesdale.

The walk through Teesdale is an easy riverside stroll. The Pennine Way roughly traces the broad meanders of the River Tees and passes through fields and beside small woods. There's

Low Force on the River Tees in the North Pennines

High Force on the River Tees in the North Pennines

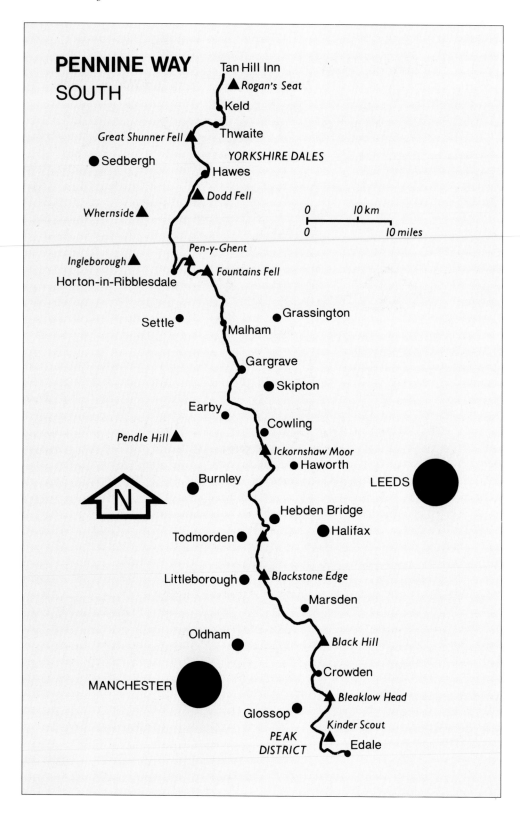

PENNINE WAY
SOUTH

Tan Hill Inn
▲ *Rogan's Seat*
● Keld
Thwaite
Great Shunner Fell ▲
YORKSHIRE DALES
● Sedbergh
● Hawes
▲ *Dodd Fell*
Whernside ▲

0   10 km
0   10 miles

Pen-y-Ghent
Ingleborough ▲
▲ *Fountains Fell*
Horton-in-Ribblesdale
● Grassington
Settle ●
Malham ●
Gargrave ●
● Skipton
Earby ●
● Cowling
Pendle Hill ▲
▲ *Ickornshaw Moor*
● Haworth
Burnley ●
LEEDS ●
Hebden Bridge
Todmorden ● ▲
● Halifax
▲ *Blackstone Edge*
Littleborough ●
Marsden
Oldham ●
▲ *Black Hill*
MANCHESTER ●
● Crowden
▲ *Bleaklow Head*
Glossop ●
Kinder Scout
PEAK
DISTRICT ▲ Edale

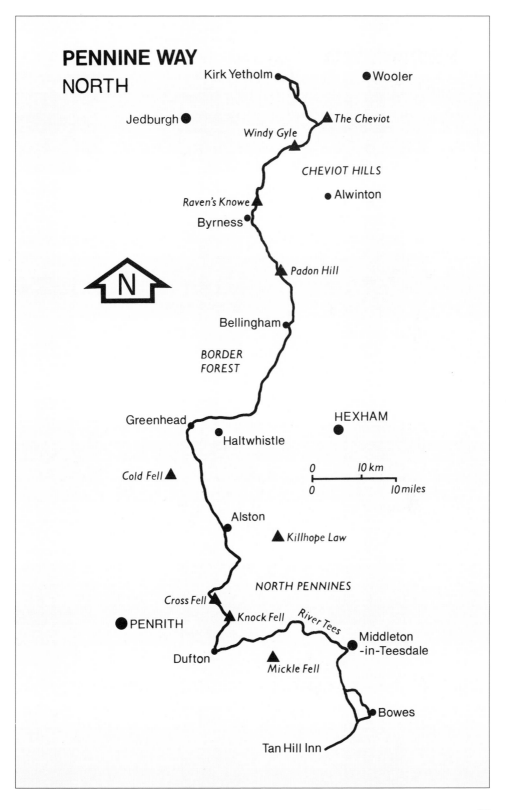

PENNINE WAY
NORTH

Kirk Yetholm • ● Wooler

Jedburgh ● ▲ The Cheviot

Windy Gyle ▲

CHEVIOT HILLS

● Alwinton

Raven's Knowe ▲
Byrness ●

▲ Padon Hill

N

Bellingham ●

*BORDER
FOREST*

Greenhead ● HEXHAM ●
● Haltwhistle

Cold Fell ▲

| 0 | 10 km |
| 0 | 10 miles |

Alston ●
▲ Killhope Law

NORTH PENNINES

Cross Fell ▲
● PENRITH ▲ Knock Fell   *River Tees*
Middleton
-in-Teesdale ●

Dufton ● ▲ Mickle Fell

● Bowes

Tan Hill Inn

a bunk-house near the trail at Holwick. Two splendid waterfalls, Low Force and High Force, are seen to good effect. The path crosses rocky ground beyond High Force and passes a large stand of juniper bushes. At Cronkley a farm access track is followed towards Langdon Beck, where a short detour reaches the youth hostel.

Langdon Beck to Dufton

14 miles (23km)

The day's trek starts easily enough, with a walk to Widdybank Farm, where teas and snacks may be available. An artificial path between the River Tees and the cliffs of Falcon Clints leads round to the spectacular cascade of Cauldron Snout. There's a huge reservoir above the fall, but the trail leads away from the dam towards the remote farmstead of Birkdale. The Pennine Way crosses bleak moorlands almost touching 600m – offering miserable walking in rain and mist. A gradual descent leads to Maize Beck and a choice of routes. If you can do it dry-shod, then ford Maize Beck and head straight for High Cup. To avoid wet feet, walk upstream to cross Maizebeck Gorge by a footbridge, then aim for High Cup.

High Cup is a magnificent steep-sided dale surrounded by a colonnaded cliff line. A path stays above the cliffs on one side, becoming quite narrow and known as the Narrowgate. A long, clear descent leads to Dufton. This charming red sandstone village has a shop, pub, youth hostel, camp-site and B & Bs.

Dufton to Alston

21 miles (34km)

A muddy walk from Dufton is followed by a long, steep and sometimes stony ascent of Knock Fell. From the large summit cairn, the trail is easy to follow in clear weather, but needs care in mist. Great Dun Fell is easily identified on account of its summit radome. Its ascent is followed by Little Dun Fell, then a boggy and bouldery climb onto the broad summit plateau of Cross Fell at 893m. This is the highest point on the Pennine Way – indeed, the highest point on any of the trails – and has a wide ranging view of northern England and southern Scotland. In foul weather, however, you'll wish you'd stayed in Dufton.

On the descent from Cross Fell, if there's any difficulty, you could seek shelter in the bothy called Greg's Hut. Sometimes, wood is left for a fire, or food for desperate wayfarers. A good mining track leads gradually downhill to Garrigill, but stays well above 500m for most of its length. There are a shop, pub, bunk-house and B & B accommodation in the village if you've had enough for one day. Hostellers have a little further to go to reach Alston, but most of the route is simply a case of following the River South Tyne. Most of Alston's shops and pubs are on a steep, cobbled street.

Alston to Greenhead

17 miles (27km)

After the big hills of yesterday's walk, today's stretch is a fairly simple plod along a valley, ending with the crossing of a low moorland. Keep your map and guide handy as there are some awkward field-paths to follow, though the way is usually marked. Leave Alston close to the River South Tyne, then climb over the spur of a hill to reach a short river walk in Gilderdale. You can inspect the remains of a Roman fort called Maiden Castle. Fiddly paths

A stout, solid, stone farmhouse on the way to Alston

lead through fields by way of Kirkhaugh to reach Slaggyford. The course of an old Roman road known as the Maiden Way leads across a dull hillside almost to Lambley.

Old colliery workings will be noticed near Lambley, then the Pennine Way wanders over the enclosed moorlands of Round Hill and Black Hill. Eventually, the trail leads across a busy road, running close to Greenhead. This is a handy place to break the journey as there are a youth hostel, camp-site and shop nearby. Technically you're leaving the Pennines, but the Pennine Way goes much further northwards to cross the Cheviot Hills too.

Greenhead to Once Brewed

8 miles (13 km)

This is quite an easy day's walk, but the course of Hadrian's Wall is something of a switchback which features some steep ascents and descents. You can take things easy during the day and spend plenty of time studying the remaining pieces of this former frontier. Some parts have vanished without trace, but other parts stand as much as 2m high. There are also forts, mile castles and turret foundations which can be discerned. Start the exploration by visiting a museum at Greenhead, then enjoy the Walltown length of Hadrian's Wall. The fort of Aesica hasn't been fully excavated, but the shapes of ruins can be distinguished beneath the turf. Another good stretch of the wall crosses Cawfield Crags, then there's a climb to 375m on Winshields Crag. After that, it's a walk down to Once Brewed Youth Hostel, near the Twice Brewed Inn, or a pitch on nearby farm camp-sites. Only backpackers should think of continuing further, as the only accommodation between Once Brewed and Bellingham is a forest camp-site.

Hadrian's Wall snakes along a rocky crest above Walltown Crags

Once Brewed to Bellingham

18 miles (29km)

The day starts with more of Hadrian's Wall – a good length over Peel Crags – then a great walk overlooking Crag Lough. After climbing over Hotbank Crags you're supposed to leave the wall at Rapishaw Gap. First, consider a short detour to the magnificent Roman fort of Housesteads. Returning to Rapishaw Gap, head towards the coniferous gloom of the enormous Wark Forest.

Throughout today and tomorrow, the trail clips the corners of one of Europe's largest plantations. Watch carefully, as the Pennine Way threads its way through, and don't be drawn along the wrong paths or tracks. After passing through this part of Wark Forest, cross Warks Burn and maybe break for a snack at Horneystead Farm. A few farms later, cross Houxty Burn and climb over Shitlington Crags before finally walking into Bellingham by road. There are a youth hostel, camp-site, shops and pubs. This is the last large range of services before the end of the walk.

Bellingham to Byrness

16 miles (26km)

The Pennine Way leaves Bellingham via a farm road and a dull moor, rather than via the scenic Hareshaw Linn and its waterfall. After crossing a road and wandering over Deer Play and Lord's Shaw, another road is crossed and the trail leads across Padon Hill. A detour would include the stony 378m summit and its pepperpot cairn.

Brownrigg Head is the last moorland summit, by which time the edge of Redesdale Forest is gained. The Pennine Way is routed along good tracks, but it's hard to gauge progress among the conifers. Eventually, the route passes Blakehopeburnhaugh and follows the River Rede to Cottonshopeburn Foot. Another forest track leads to Byrness. This little village has a youth hostel, camp-site, hotel and shop. You need to consider carefully your plans for tomorrow, as the Cheviots are the broadest and bleakest part of the trail.

Byrness to Uswayford

16 miles (26km)

The last leg of the Pennine Way is tough and needs to be planned carefully. It's 29 miles (47km) from Byrness to Kirk Yetholm and few walkers would want to complete that in a single day. The ground is consistently high and underfoot it can be wet and boggy. In bad weather the walk can seem like a treadmill. If you're carrying a tent you'll be able to pitch it somewhere along the way. The only shelter available in bad weather is a refuge hut before Lamb Hill and an old railway carriage shelter below Auchope Cairn. The only accommodation is off-route at Uswayford and this remote B & B must be booked in advance.

The Pennine Way leaves Byrness and climbs up a forested slope onto Byrness Hill. Stay close to the forest fence to reach Coquet Head, then head towards the ancient Roman camps at Chew Green. For the rest of the day the route stays high on the crest of the Cheviot Hills and usually follows the Border Fence between England and Scotland. Note the hut which occurs before 511m Lamb Hill. There are a series of easy ascents beyond, with boggy patches, before a steeper climb to the 619m summit of Windy Gyle. Sometimes, there are crude shelters on the boulder-strewn part of the hill. Your options are as follows: continue to Kirk Yetholm; continue to the old railway carriage below Auchope Cairn; or descend to Uswayford for B & B accommodation. The last option involves following a path eastwards between recent forestry plantations to reach the farm.

Uswayford to Kirk Yetholm

16 miles (26km)

In the morning you'll have to climb uphill from Uswayford to rejoin the Pennine Way near Windy Gyle. Again, the Border Fence provides a sure guide along the broad and boggy moorland crest. There's a climb to the top of Auchope Cairn, then a detour through appalling bogs simply to visit the 815m summit of The Cheviot. Many walkers omit this summit and go straight over Auchope Cairn to pass the railway carriage shelter far below.

The fence continues close to the 605m summit of The Schil. Cross over into Scotland and beyond Black Hag there's a choice of routes. The original course of the Pennine Way

(*overleaf*) **Uswayford – a remote farmhouse B & B, a little way off the Cheviot crest**

was a simple descent to Burnhead and a walk along the valley road. Another route now allows walkers to stay high on the hills to reach White Law before descending to the valley road. Either way, a short road walk leads over to Kirk Yetholm. The walk is over and traditionally ends at the bar of the Border Hotel. A youth hostel and camp-site are available.

PENNINE WAY INFORMATION

Schedule:	miles	km
Edale – Crowden YH	17	27
Crowden – Standedge IH	13	21
Standedge – Mankinholes YH	13	21
Mankinholes – Ponden Hall BB	15	24
Ponden Hall – Gargrave BB	17	27
Gargrave – Horton BB	21	34
Horton – Hawes YH	15	24
Hawes – Keld YH	13	21
Keld – Baldersdale YH	15	24
Baldersdale – Langdon Beck YH	15	24
Langdon Beck – Dufton YH	14	23
Dufton – Alston YH	21	34
Alston – Greenhead YH	17	27
Greenhead – Once Brewed YH	8	13
Once Brewed – Bellingham YH	18	29
Bellingham – Byrness YH	16	26
Byrness – Uswayford BB	16	26
Uswayford – Kirk Yetholm YH	16	26
Total distance	280	451

Maps:
OSGB 1:50,000 Landranger Sheets 74, 80, 86, 91, 92, 98, 103, 109 & 110.

Guidebooks:
National Trail Guides, Pennine Way South and *Pennine Way North*, both by Tony Hopkins, published by the Countryside Commission, Ordnance Survey and Aurum Press Ltd. *Pennine Way Companion*, by A Wainwright, published by Michael Joseph Ltd. *A Guide to the Pennine Way*, by C J Wright, published by Constable & Co Ltd. *Pennine Way part one* and *Pennine Way part two*, combined map/guides published by Footprint.

Accommodation List:
The Pennine Way Association.

Path Association:
The Pennine Way Association.

Tourist Information Centres:
Edale, Hebden Bridge, Haworth, Colne, Skipton, Malham, Horton, Hawes, Middleton, Alston, Haltwhistle, Bellingham, Kelso.

Wales

◆

The Pembrokeshire Coast Path

When the Pembrokeshire Coast National Park was designated, one of the park authority's first moves was to look into the possibility of a long-distance walking route around the coast of south-west Wales. Almost all of Pembrokeshire's coast is made up of low cliffs contorted into an endless succession of headlands and bays. A spread of islands and stacks add considerable interest to seaward views and prove to be popular with many species of birds.

If you could unravel the coast path from St Dogmaels to Amroth, you'd find it was equal in length to the Offa's Dyke Path, yet it fits neatly into a small corner of Wales. Pembrokeshire is divided into two parts by a line you could identify on the map – the Landsker. The northern area mostly features Welsh place names, while the southern parts seem predominantly English. The area was half-settled by the Normans and the division has lasted for centuries. Coastal signposts are usually bilingual – reading 'Coast Path' and 'Llwybr Arfordir'. You'll also notice that most of the stiles are numbered, and there are nearly five hundred of them!

The walk is usually fairly easy, but there are some short, steep sections and a number of rugged areas. There are several youth hostels, but they are unevenly spaced and you would need to fall back on B & B provision to fill any lengthy gaps. Camp-sites are abundant and backpacking is certainly worth considering. Many parts of the coast are popular and you can

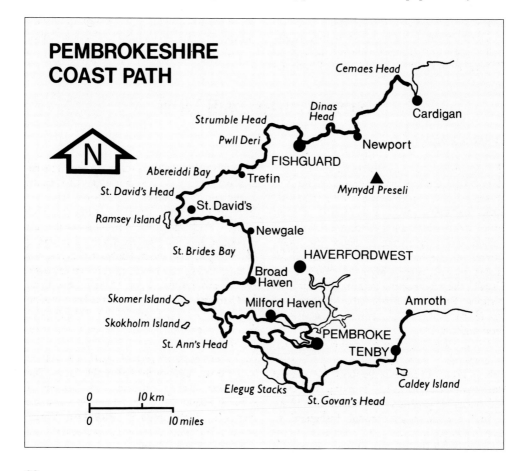

expect to find shops and cafes, but some stretches have very few facilities. There's one urban and industrial part, around Milford Haven. Some walkers catch a bus round this inlet, saving 35 miles (55km) of walking. The total distance of the coast path is 180 miles (290km), so it would take anything up to a fortnight to complete.

There's some information you need to obtain the moment you start making your plans. The extensive Castlemartin Range is used for live firing and can be closed to walkers. Local tourist information offices will be able to give you details of clear periods when the range is open. It's best to plan your entire route around the availability of Range East being open, as that part is really too good to miss. You could also walk through Range West from time to time, but only on one of the guided walks arranged by the national park authority.

St Dogmaels to Newport

15 miles (24km)

If you start walking late from St Dogmaels, near Cardigan, you'll find a youth hostel and places to camp above Poppit Sands. There's a cafe nearby, and a pub proclaiming itself to be the last pub before Ireland. The coast path follows a road at first, then takes a path round Cemaes Head. You climb as high as 175m and this is the highest part of the trail.

There are plenty of ups and downs as the walk progresses. There's a steep descent to Ceibwr Bay and the formation of Pwll y Wrach is passed later. At this point, the sea has undercut the cliff path and excavated a deep pool on the opposite side. The route gradually climbs high above rugged slopes and after rounding a number of headlands there's suddenly a view of Newport. A shore walk leads to a bridge over the Afon Nyfer, then a detour into town allows you to find B & B accommodation or visit the shops, pubs and cafes. There's a camp-site nearby.

Newport to Pwll Deri

21 miles (34km)

It's a very crinkly coastline beyond Newport, but you can gauge your progress by looking ahead to Dinas Head. When the lovely little village of Cwm-yr-Eglwys is reached, you can either walk around Dinas Head, or short cut behind it to Pwllgwaelod. From the 142m summit of the headland the view inland includes the low, rugged Mynydd Preseli range. Usually, the extent of the Pembrokeshire Coast National Park is no further than you can see inland. At Pwllgwaelod, there's a pub serving food and drink.

The coast path continues with plenty of ins, outs, ups and downs, passing a camp-site with a shop. Look out for Needle Rock – a pointed stack with a hole to justify its name. The cliffs and stacks are profusely populated with birds. It takes a while to get through Fishguard, as there's a descent to Lower Town, then a cliff walk around the higher part of town. Fishguard has a full range of services if you want to break this long day's walk and continue to the youth hostels of Pwll Deri or Trefin tomorrow.

A promenade walk leads to Goodwick, from where a ferry sails to Ireland. This is the last chance to buy food before Trefin. The trail is fairly easy at first above Harbour Heights, but it starts to hug the headlands and makes wide sweeps around little bays. There's a memorial on Carregwastad Point where the last invasion of Britain took place in 1797. The French force didn't get far and after skirmishes a treaty was concluded at Fishguard. If you lose track of your exact position on this crinkly coast, then look for the lighthouse at Strumble Head. The coast path takes in some fine rocky scenery as it turns round the point, then after a while there's a climb uphill to Pwll Deri Youth Hostel. This place is superbly sited and there's also a camp-site nearby.

Pwll Deri to St David's

20 miles (32km)

After a rugged start, the trail turns a point at Penbwchdy and descends to Pwllcrochan. After wandering around the bays of Aber Bach and Aber Mawr there's a climb towards the fine headlands of Penmorfa and Trwyn Llwynog. Later, there's a stout wall alongside the path which has been amusingly inscribed as 'The Great Wall of China'. After turning another headland there's a descent to the delightful little harbour of Abercastle. A series of splendid headlands are passed before the path descends to Aber Draw. Trefin is just off-route, where there are a youth hostel, shop and pub.

After walking to Porth-gain, a former industrial harbour, a break could be taken at a handy pub. A series of jagged headlands are quite complex, but the coast path tends to keep well away from them. A fairly easy path leads onwards to Abereiddi, where curious landforms are entirely the result of quarrying. The village is in ruins, though there might be a snacks van parked on the beach.

The trail becomes, by degrees, more difficult. Steep, rocky slopes clothed in scrub fall seawards. Watch carefully as the path picks its way across the slopes, as it becomes vague in places. There's no mistaking St David's Head, where a significant turning has to be made. Eventually, the route reaches Whitesands Bay, where there are a cafe and camp-site. St David's Youth Hostel isn't too far inland.

St David's to Broad Haven

24 miles (39km)

The coast path continues around Whitesands Bay and seaward views feature Ramsey Island. Boats sometimes run to the island from St Justinian's. A walk around a headland comes quite close to Ramsey Island, but once around the point the enormous sweep of St Bride's Bay comes into view. The trail leads around a succession of small bays and headlands. There's Porthlysgi Bay, then the narrow Porth Clais, followed by St Non's Bay where St David was born. The 'Cathedral City' of St David's is further inland. After Caerfai Bay and Caer Bwdy Bay the path begins to miss out most of the intricate ins and outs and heads more directly to Solva.

Solva lies alongside a pronounced crooked inlet. It's a popular place where you can get food and drink before moving on. Leave by walking along a narrow, steep-sided ridge, then walk round a bay to reach the rugged point of Dinas Fawr. It's possible to walk along this spine of rock, but you would have to retrace your steps to continue. There's a switchback section to cover before reaching Newgale, where the route crosses the Landsker – from the Welsh part of Pembrokeshire into 'Little England'.

There's B & B accommodation and camp-site at Newgale if you want to break this long day's walk, but the nearest youth hostel is at Broad Haven. To reach it, walk alongside the sandy beach, then cross an involved series of little headlands until there's a final descent to Broad Haven.

Broad Haven to Marloes Sands

13 miles (21km)

A steep road links Broad Haven with Little Haven and you won't find any more shops and pubs on today's walk. The trail is easy as it progresses around Borough Head, passing Mill Haven to reach St Bride's Haven. After turning around The Nab Head and walking round a broad bay, the coast path reaches the Deer Park. This walled off headland was once the site of an ancient promontory fort and you have the option of walking all the way round it. There are sometimes boat trips to Skomer and Skokholm Islands – both important nature reserves. There's even an undersea nature reserve (Lundy Island is another one). Information about the Dyfed Wildlife Trust, who manage the reserves, is available from a small hut nearby. Sweets, drinks and souvenirs are on sale too.

An attractive cliff walk leads past Gateholm Island, which can be reached on foot when the tide is out. After that comes the broad sweep of Marloes Sands. A short walk inland leads to Marloes Sands Youth Hostel. Like St David's, the hostel is spread around a number of former farm buildings. In the evening, you need to study a set of tidetables for tomorrow's walk.

Marloes Sands to Milford Haven

19 miles (30km)

A fairly easy coastal walk leaves Marloes Sands and goes round a disused airfield before dropping down to Westdale Bay. If you need to save some time, you could short cut to the village of Dale. However, the walk around St Ann's Head is more interesting and scenic, ending with a road walk into Dale. Some walkers will catch the bus between Dale and Angle to avoid walking round the enormous inlet of Milford Haven. The mouth of Milford Haven is only 1½ miles (2km) wide, but it's going to take two days to walk round it.

To proceed beyond Dale, you need to be walking while the tide is out. A little footbridge crosses the channel of The Gann, then a beach walk leads to Musselwick where a path on dry land can be followed. There's a fine cliff walk round Lindsway Bay, then there are circuits around Great and Little Castle Heads. Again, while the tide is out, there are stepping stones across the channel of Sandyhaven Pill. After passing a camp-site a large embankment screens walkers from a view of a former oil refinery site. Long jetties project seawards before Gelliswick Bay. The town of Milford Haven lies just beyond and offers a range of shops, pubs and accommodation. A visitor centre by the harbour explains all about the industry of the area.

A solid sea fort guards the entrance to the inlet of Milford Haven

Milford Haven to Angle

23 miles (37km)

When you've looked on the eyesores of Milford Haven, you'll be able to appreciate the beauty spots all the more. There's a short detour away from the sea at the start of the day's walk, then a coastal path is found close to an oil refinery. Two footbridges enclosed in mesh cages could be unnerving for vertigo sufferers to cross, but there's no alternative route.

The pleasant village of Llanstadwell is followed by the dormitory village of Neyland and a wooded walk to a high-level bridge. A busy road is followed across two bridges spanning the tidal inlets of the Daugleddau, then roads are followed through Pembroke Dock, passing another ferry port for Ireland. Roads and field-paths lead over to Pembroke, which is a fine little town dominated by a huge castle worth exploring.

The route from Pembroke to Pwllcrochan is hardly coastal, but wanders along roads or links farms by paths and tracks. After passing huge pylons and a farm serving teas, a power station is passed. Beyond Pwllcrochan a coastal path skirts one last oil refinery. The tide needs to be out for a beach walk to Angle. At this little village, the industrial interlude is over. There are shops, pubs, cafes, B & Bs and a camp-site.

Angle to Bosherston

18 miles (29km)

The trail leads around a headland from Angle Bay to West Angle Bay. There is a view back across the great inlet of Milford Haven, then the route turns to face the wilder parts of the Pembrokeshire coast once more. A path wanders along cliffs, skirting a small military area and passing small headlands and bays. A descent leads to a wide sweep of sand dunes. Ahead lie the extensive Castlemartin Ranges.

Range West is reached first and there's no access for walkers except on one of the few guided walks arranged by the national park authority each year. The coast path is nowhere near the coast, but follows a road inland to the village of Castlemartin. Food and drink are available at the Blue Chick Inn. If there's any firing on Range East, you'll have no alternative but to follow minor roads to Bosherston.

If Range East is open, then follow roads signposted for Elegug Stacks. These splendid stacks and cliffs are most attractive and an arch known as the Green Bridge of Wales can also be studied. The area is rich in birdlife too. The coast path continues along the top of the cliffs, passing headlands which are sometimes punctured by caves and arches. A flight of steps can later be followed down to St Govan's Chapel and Holy Wells. After walking round St Govan's Head to Broad Haven, a short walk inland leads to the little village of Bosherston. There is a pub and limited B & B accommodation.

Bosherston to Manorbier

14 miles (23km)

The coast path leaves the beach of Broad Haven, near Bosherston, and goes round Stackpole Head and Barafundle Bay to reach the tiny Stackpole Quay. After rounding Greenala Point and Trewent Point the route descends to the beach at Freshwater East. Houses and chalets are stacked up a steep slope, but there are places down by the beach where you can get things to eat and drink. Watch carefully for the course of the path as it climbs back on to the higher cliffs. After walking round Swanlake Bay and Manorbier Bay the coast path approaches

Stone steps lead down to St Govan's Chapel in a limestone cleft

Old Castle Head. There's a detour inland at this point to avoid a military site on the headland. Manorbier village has shops, pubs, B & Bs and a nearby camp-site, while the youth hostel is a little further along the coast at Shrinkle Haven. It's been developed from a former military building and now looks quite striking.

Manorbier to Amroth

15 miles (24km)

Caldey Island is prominently in view at the start of this day's walk. After walking around Lydstep Point and Lydstep Haven you might have to make a detour inland as there's a firing range on a rocky point near Penally. On non-firing days walkers are allowed round the point before descending to the beach, while at other times you are routed through the village instead. If the tide permits, then the best way to reach Tenby is to walk along the sandy beach. High tides would force you behind a dune belt to walk alongside a railway instead.

Tenby is finely situated on a rocky headland and has some splendid old buildings within the remains of its old walls. Go through the walls at the Five Arches and you'll have access to a full range of services in this popular resort. To leave town, the trail heads slightly inland, returning to the cliff line at Waterwynch. Watch carefully for the line of the path when crossing the deeply cut, wooded Lodge Valley. The route follows a switchback course, going round a point and crossing another wooded valley. There are a number of routes available at Saundersfoot. If the tides permit, you can walk on the beach. If rock falls permit, you can walk through a series of old railway tunnels. If neither route is available, then there's a cliff top path too. All the routes reach Wiseman's Bridge.

There's another move inland as you climb up from Wiseman's Bridge, then the path leads back towards the coast. There's a steep descent to Amroth – a small village with just enough services to make it a good place to end the walk. Technically, the Pembrokeshire Coast Path continues along the road to end at a bridge near Amroth Castle. If you're stuck for accommodation, buses head back into Tenby, or to Pentlepoir Youth Hostel.

PEMBROKESHIRE COAST PATH INFORMATION

Schedule:	miles	km
St Dogmaels – Newport BB	15	24
Newport – Pwll Deri YH	21	34
Pwll Deri – St David's YH	20	32
St David's – Broad Haven YH	24	39
Broad Haven – Marloes Sands YH	13	21
Marloes Sands – Milford Haven BB	19	30
Milford Haven – Angle BB	23	37
Angle – Bosherston BB	18	29
Bosherston – Manorbier YH	14	23
Manorbier – Amroth for YH	15	24
Total distance	182	293

Maps:
OSGB 1:50,000 Landranger Sheets 145, 157 & 158.

Guidebooks:
National Trail Guide, Pembrokeshire Coast Path, by Brian John, published by the Countryside Commission, Ordnance Survey and Aurum Press Ltd. *A Guide to the Pembrokeshire Coast Path*, by C J Wright, published by Constable & Co Ltd. *The Pembrokeshire Coast Path*, by John Merrill, published by JNM Publications.

Accommodation List:
Pembrokeshire Coast National Park Authority.

Tourist Information Centres:
Cardigan, Newport, Fishguard, St David's, Broad Haven, Haverfordwest, Milford Haven, Pembroke, Tenby, Saundersfoot.

The end of the coastal walk – the village of Amroth

The Offa's Dyke Path (map p.108)

When Offa, King of Mercia, raised his awesome dyke, he didn't realise that he was laying the foundations of a long-distance walking route. There are no contemporary records relating to the construction of this great earthwork, but later accounts and archaeological excavations point to the eighth century. Some of the dyke is quite evident, other parts are traceable, and some of it has been obliterated, if it ever existed. Even its purpose is unclear – it may have been a boundary mark, or it may have been a defensive structure, or even a frontier that could be controlled. The best thing prospective walkers could do is to visit the Offa's Dyke Heritage Centre at Knighton and take on board all the opinions about the dyke's history and purpose.

Let's get this straight at the outset – the Offa's Dyke Path doesn't always follow Offa's Dyke, and Offa's Dyke hardly ever coincides with the current Anglo-Welsh border. Less than a third of the path's 177 miles (285km) traces Offa's Dyke, but for odd, short stretches the path, dyke and border all pursue the same course. The route you'll be following runs from coast to coast through the Welsh Marches from Chepstow to Prestatyn. You'll be crossing the border from time to time, but you won't notice unless you're watching your map and guide carefully. The countryside traversed is remarkably varied and includes open hills, cultivated fields, riverside, forest and woodland walks. Several small towns and villages are visited. The Offa's Dyke Path goes through the Brecon Beacons National Park, as well as the Wye Valley, Shropshire Hills and Clwydian Range Areas of Outstanding Natural Beauty.

The walk varies from easy to difficult. In some places the path is firm, but in other places it can be muddy. The walk through the Black Mountains, on the edge of the Brecon Beacons, can be featureless in rain and mist. You'll need to be fit and agile as there are reckoned to be about seven hundred stiles to climb. Heavily laden walkers, clad in waterproofs and covered in mud will soon tire of all these hurdles. Youth hostel accommodation is sparse, with some addresses being too far off-route. B & Bs are numerous and backpacking is a worthy option as there are several small camp-sites available. It's a good idea to reserve time to explore castles, abbeys and other borderland ruins.

Sedbury Cliff to Monmouth

18 miles (29km)

Chepstow is easily reached, but Sedbury Cliff is rather an awkward place to start a walk. However you get there, the walk starts above the Severn Estuary, right on the course of Offa's Dyke. The course of the dyke is soon lost in Sedbury, but it crops up throughout the day's walk. The route is never far from the River Wye and there are occasional views across its broad, deeply incised meanders. The path stays fairly high above Tintern on a wooded slope, offering a bird's-eye view of Tintern Abbey. Two alternative routes later present themselves. One traces the River Wye further upstream, while the other stays faithful to the scanty course of Offa's Dyke. The latter choice crosses St Briavel's Common and anyone staying at St Briavel's Youth Hostel will take that course. The hostel is housed in a splendid castle.

Both routes join at Bigsweir, then the trail climbs high above the Wye, wandering through woods and over high pastures before descending to Redbrook and its pubs. The final climb of the day reaches the Naval Temple and Round House, from where there are good views over Monmouth. A gradual descent leads to the town, which has a full range of facilities. There are several notable buildings and a fine old gatehouse on Monnow Bridge.

Monmouth to Pandy

17 miles (27km)

The countryside between Monmouth and Pandy is low lying and pleasant, but largely unremarkable. You'll see nothing of Offa's Dyke for days. There are abundant stiles and the path can be muddy. There are charming little hamlets and the occasional pub. Little churches are worth visiting – the most romantically dedicated being Llanfihangel Ystum Llywern, or St Michael's of the Fiery Meteor. Llantilio Crosseny has another fine church, plus a pub called The Hostry. Look out for a view of Ysgyryd Fawr – a hill whose summit is said to have been cleft by the keel of Noah's Ark.

The extensive ruins of White Castle are passed on a low hill. Three castles controlled the Marches in this area and there is an unofficial Castles Alternative which runs parallel to the Offa's Dyke Path. The Black Mountains rise in the distance, but there are many more stiles to cross before you reach their open slopes. The little village of Llangattocklingoed has a pub and bunk-house. Pandy is the last place before the Black Mountains and has a pub, a small choice of B & Bs or small camp-sites.

Pandy to Hay-On-Wye

17 miles (27km)

The finest, or worst day on the Offa's Dyke Path depends on the type of weather experienced in the Black Mountains. In desperation you could drop down to Capel-y-ffin, where there's a youth hostel. The climb from Pandy to the broad moorland crest is fairly easy. A well trodden path is routed along the crest, but it can be muddy in places. The path roughly traces the border between Wales and England. Everything on the Welsh side is in the Brecon Beacons National Park. In fine weather this is a great walk with wide ranging views. In foul weather it's a treadmill and the only way to chart your progress is to note the four widely spaced trig points which have been planted along the crest. The highest stands at 703m and this is the most elevated point gained on the Offa's Dyke Path.

The last trig point stands on the broad rise of Hay Bluff, where you could have a fine view of the country ahead. A prominent path leads down the steep face of the hill, then gentle walking continues down to Hay-on-Wye. This little town is just inside Wales and is well worth exploring. It has many fine buildings, including a castle. The castle is full of books, and most of the shops in town sell second-hand books. If you're the bookshop browsing type, then you'd better enquire about weekly rates at one of the B & Bs in town.

Hay-On-Wye to Kington

15 miles (24km)

Follow the River Wye downstream from Hay, which is odd when you think you were following it upstream from Chepstow. The Black Mountains remain in view, but the surrounding countryside seems tame. Low, hilly country gradually increases in height. The wooded Bettws Dingle is followed by an easy walk over Little Mountain. You'll probably be unaware of a brief incursion into England, but the route is back into Wales before reaching Newchurch. Look for the timbered Great House on the way into the village.

Good views are available from the 383m Disgwylfa Hill, then a gradual descent leads to Gladestry, where there are a shop and pub. The steep end of Hergest Ridge frowns on the little

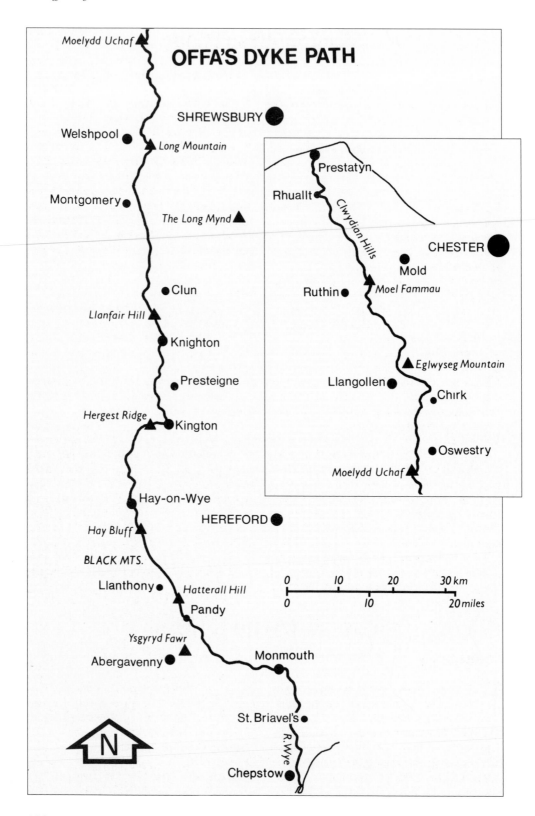

OFFA'S DYKE PATH

Moelydd Uchaf

SHREWSBURY

Welshpool

Long Mountain

Montgomery

The Long Mynd

Clun

Llanfair Hill

Knighton

Presteigne

Hergest Ridge

Kington

Hay-on-Wye

HEREFORD

Hay Bluff

BLACK MTS.

Llanthony

Hatterall Hill

Pandy

Ysgyryd Fawr

Abergavenny

Monmouth

St. Briavel's

R. Wye

N

Chepstow

Prestatyn

Rhuallt

Clwydian Hills

CHESTER

Mold

Ruthin

Moel Fammau

Eglwyseg Mountain

Llangollen

Chirk

Oswestry

Moelydd Uchaf

0	10	20	30 km
0		10	20 miles

village, but the trail uses a clear track to make a fairly easy ascent. The walk along the grassy, bracken-covered hill touches 420m before going down alongside an old racecourse to reach Kington. The route has crossed into England again – though that counts for little in the Marches. Note the fine buildings, narrow streets, cluttered appearance, small shops and central clock tower. This is a typical Marches town and the style will be repeated at other points along the trail.

Kington to Knighton

14 miles (23km)

There's a climb into a hilly region above Kington and traces of Offa's Dyke are found on Herrock Hill. The trail leads back into Wales, and more traces of the dyke are found around Burfa. It's a fairly plain feature as it crosses Evenjobb Hill, then quite unmistakable as it tears across the crest of low hills before descending to Dolley. After crossing a river you climb up Furrow Hill to find the next length of the dyke. It's easily followed over Hawthorn Hill, then, after an interruption, its course is clear over one last hill before descending to Knighton.

Knighton has a full range of facilities, including a youth hostel. The hostel is in an old school, which also houses the Offa's Dyke Heritage Centre and local tourist information centre. You should be able to get your questions answered about the dyke. The Offa's Dyke Association is also based here, so if there's anything you need to know about the walk, then just ask. Down by the river is a stone marking the point where the trail was officially opened. Knighton is generally regarded as the halfway point, which isn't strictly true, but the best of Offa's Dyke is yet to be revealed.

The hump of the Hergest Ridge rises above the village of Gladestry

Knighton to Montgomery

19 miles (31km)

The whole day's walk is remarkably faithful to the course of Offa's Dyke. There's hardly anything to see on the steep climb away from Knighton, which is wholly in England. The earthwork increases in stature as it progresses through the Shropshire Hills and becomes monumental on Llanfair Hill. This is also known as the High Dyke and it can often be traced clearly in distant views. You can specu-late on what determined the choice of route – sometimes on one side of a hill, sometimes over the top. Some of the switchback sections could prove quite tiring. Churchtown is a tiny hamlet with nothing to offer passing wayfarers, but it's memorable for the long, steep descent and subsequent reascent while crossing the valley.

After a breather, the next valley is taken at a gentler gradient, then the trail crosses the

The path leads past the beautifully timbered house of Bryndrinog

Montgomery to Llanymynech

21 miles (34km)

Offa's Dyke continues to be traced across fields from Montgomery. It can be followed across low hills to Forden, then runs across the foot of Long Mountain. The Offa's Dyke Path, however, climbs to the 408m summit of the hill. It rises through forests, samples the view, then descends through fields to reach Buttington and a pub. Beyond Buttington the Montgomery Canal is joined and its tow-path is followed to Pool Quay. Maintaining a watery theme, the trail crosses a road and follows an embankment alongside the River Severn. There's a detour away from the river later so that an odd length of Offa's Dyke can be traced to Four Crosses. As the dyke leading to Llanymynech is under a busy tarmac road, the trail again takes advantage of the tow-path of the Montgomery Canal to reach the village. Despite its small size, Llanymynech has shops, pubs, B & Bs and nearby camp-sites.

Llanymynech to Froncysyllte

18 miles (29km)

After leaving Llanymynech, Offa's Dyke can be followed around the edge of Llanymynech Hill and the trail crosses from Wales to England. Although the dyke leads across another hill, the trail goes instead over 285m Moel Uchaf. After descending to the village of Trefonen, where there are shops and pubs, the line of the dyke is joined again. The route crosses the steep-sided, wooded Candy Valley and crosses an old racecourse. Again, the trail has drifted away from the dyke, but joins it again to cross some low hills. There follows another stretch where the path, dyke and border pursue a common course over a switch-back of little hills.

Kerry Ridgeway and finally descends to the plains. Even though a patchwork of fields covers the dyke, you should be able to trace its course with certainty even from a distance. Mellington Hall looks impressive from afar, but it is later shielded behind trees. The Blue Bell Inn at Brompton Crossroads is handy for a break. The last part of the day's walk features the path, dyke and border, all perfectly aligned. A short detour off-route to Montgomery provides walkers with a range of services including shops, pubs, B & Bs and nearby camp-sites.

One of many hundreds of stiles, but not all are fringed with lovely snowdrops

There are two routes from Castle Mill and the rest of the trail runs through Wales. In the summer it's possible to walk fairly close to Chirk Castle, but at other times a line further west has to be followed. Paths and roads lead down towards the River Dee, where the last part of Offa's Dyke is followed. No traces will be seen of it for the rest of the walk. The tow-path of the Llangollen Canal leads to Froncysyllte, which has shops, pubs, B & Bs and a camp-site. A bus ride could take hostellers to Llangollen Youth Hostel.

Froncysyllte to Llandegla

11 miles (18km)

There are two ways to cross the River Dee. Either follow the road, or cross the canal aqueduct. The latter course isn't recommended for vertigo sufferers, and children or dogs could easily slip between the widely spaced bars alongside the narrow tow-path. After climbing gently uphill through woodlands the trail emerges on a narrow tarmac road known as the Panorama Walk. There are tremendous views across the Vale of Llangollen and upwards to striking rocky edges. The road crosses a gap between the main escarpment and the isolated Castell Dinas Bran which is crowned with an ancient hill-fort. The road continues across the steep, stony hillside to reach Rock Farm.

Beyond Rock Farm a path leads across the rugged limestone slopes. This is an excellent route with great scenery, eventually entering woodlands at World's End. A road leads uphill through the woods and crosses a high moorland. A boggy path leads away from the road and climbs up the moorland slope to reach a forest. A well trodden path descends through the forest and the trail leads to the little villages of Pen-y-Stryt and Llandegla. There is B & B and camp-site accommodation at Llandegla. Anyone continuing further would be faced with a long walk to the next lodgings.

Llandegla to Bodfari

18 miles (29km)

Keep an eye on your map and guide after leaving Llandegla as many fields have to be crossed on fiddly paths. The trail leads uphill by degrees to reach the first of the Clwydian Range. At first, the Offa's Dyke Path avoids the actual summits, keeping to the slopes of Moel y Gelli, Moel y Plas, Moel Llanfair and Moel Gyw. There are good views across the Vale of Clwyd to Snowdonia. At Clwyd Gate you can break for food and drink. Maeshafn Youth Hostel is some distance off-route, but can be reached from this gap.

The trail continues to avoid the summits, keeping low on Moel Eithinen and Foel Fenlli. There's a steep descent to a road, then a broad track leads all the way to the 554m summit of Moel Fammau. One side of the Clwydian Range is forested, while the other side is open moorland. A ruined tower on the summit of Moel Fammau has been equipped with view indicators. Having gained one summit, the trail stays high over Moel Dywyli and Moel Llys-y-coed. There's a steep descent to cross a road, then a steep climb around Moel Arthur. This hill has a summit fort, while a larger enclosure crowns Penycloddiau. A long and gradual descent leads to Bodfari, where you'll find food, drink, B & Bs and a camp-site.

Bodfari to Prestatyn

12 miles (19km)

Minor roads, tracks and paths lead away from Bodfari, gradually crossing high fields on Cefn Du. Eventually, the route heads down to Rhuallt and crosses a busy road via a footbridge. You could break for a drink and snack at Rhuallt, or continue to Prestatyn. The Offa's Dyke Path climbs uphill and passes the forested Mynydd y Cwm. Field-paths lead over Marian Ffrith and past Henfryn Hall to reach a sudden steep slope. Keep high on this final edge, which offers a bird's-eye view of Prestatyn. Eventually, a path descends diagonally across the steep slope and all that remains is a walk along the road, straight through town to end on the beach amid all the trappings of a seaside resort.

OFFA'S DYKE PATH INFORMATION

Schedule:

	miles	*km*
Sedbury Cliff – Monmouth YH	18	29
Monmouth – Pandy BB	17	27
Pandy – Hay-on-Wye BB	17	27
Hay-on-Wye – Kington BB	15	24
Kington – Knighton YH	14	23
Knighton – Montgomery BB	19	31
Montgomery – Llanymynech BB	21	34
Llanymynech – Froncysyllte BB	18	29
Froncysyllte – Llandegla BB	11	18
Llandegla – Bodfari BB	18	29
Bodfari – Prestatyn BB	12	19
Total distance	180	290

Maps:

OSGB 1:50,000 Landranger Sheets 116, 117, 126, 137, 148, 161 & 162.

Guidebooks:

National Trail Guides, Offa's Dyke Path South and *Offa's Dyke Path North*, both by Ernie and Kathy Kay and Mark Richards, published by the Countryside Commission, Ordnance Survey and Aurum Press Ltd. *A Guide to Offa's Dyke Path*, by C J Wright, published by Constable & Co Ltd.

Accommodation List:

The Offa's Dyke Association.

Path Association:

The Offa's Dyke Association.

Tourist Information Centres:

Chepstow, Monmouth, Hay-on-Wye, Kington, Knighton, Welshpool, Oswestry, Llangollen, Ruthin, Prestatyn.

Scotland

◆

The Southern Upland Way

(map pp.120–1)

The Southern Upland Way is a coast to coast trail across southern Scotland, from Portpatrick to Cockburnspath. It's a very varied walk, with low-lying stretches and ranges of hills, open moorlands and enclosed pastures, forest tracks and lakeside paths, with short coastal walks at either end. Although there are several towns and villages along the way, there are lengthy stretches away from habitation. In bad weather some parts could be difficult. A significant part of the 212 miles (341km) is along hard forest tracks or minor roads, so this is a notorious walk for blisters.

You need to give considerable thought to accommodation along the Southern Upland Way. There are only a handful of youth hostels, and some of them are off-route. B & Bs are fairly plentiful, but unevenly spread and in some places limited to a single address. Again, you may have to wander off-route to find them. There are a few odd bothies, placed in remote areas where you might be glad of the emergency lodgings they offer. Usually, there's wood for making a fire and previous walkers may have left a bit of food for you. It's on a route such as this that backpacking should be given serious consideration. There are a few organised sites, a number of small, informal sites, or places where you could establish discreet wild camps. Small villages along the way usually have a couple of shops and pubs, but you need to know where your next supplies can be obtained and you need to carry enough to sustain you in case of benightedness in remote areas.

These warnings aren't intended to discourage you, but rather to encourage you to think ahead. If your plans are well laid you can concentrate on enjoying the walk across Scotland. The scenes offer varied wildlife habitats and some of the towns and villages amply reward a short exploration. History and heritage are often well displayed, whether you're looking at numerous Covenanter memorials or the large open-air mining museum at Wanlockhead. It would take up to a fortnight to complete the route.

Looking across Loch Trool towards the bleak Galloway Hills

Portpatrick to New Luce

23 miles (37km)

Portpatrick is a little village huddled around a small harbour. It used to be a major link with Ireland, but most traffic goes through Stranraer these days. The little streets are worth exploring if you spend a night there. An easy coastal walk leaves Portpatrick, but the way becomes more difficult before Black Head is reached. Turn inland to follow quiet roads to Knock and Maize. An area of low moorland is crossed and a small reservoir is noted. If you're starting the walk late in the day, then you could aim for Stranraer for a night's accommodation and head for New Luce the next day.

Minor roads and tracks lead across almost level land to reach Castle Kennedy. There are a shop and hotel in the village if you need anything to eat or drink. If not, then cross a road and walk through ornamental grounds along the shores of White Loch. After a short road walk a farm road leads close to the fine farmhouse of Chlenry.

The route above Chlenry could go one of two ways. The official line runs through a large forest and is fully waymarked, but it's closed until a footbridge is built over a railway line. There's already a fine suspension footbridge over the Water of Luce near Galdenoch. Until the railway bridge appears, walkers are diverted along a minor road to New Luce. This village has a few B & Bs, a camp-site, shop and pub.

New Luce to Bargrennan

17 miles (27km)

The official route follows a track which climbs to Kilhern, before descending to a waterfall near Barnshangan. Walkers who have diverted into New Luce simply follow a road up to the waterfall. Continue along the road, gradually climbing past a high farm and following a track onto extensive enclosed moorlands. Keep an eye open for widely spaced waymarks in mist.

There is a large area of forest spread across the moors around Craigairie Fell. The Southern Upland Way is routed along a variety of tracks, paths and rides, so watch for waymarks all the way through. There's a clearing at Laggangarn where two standing stones have been planted, then later a slight detour can be made to inspect The Wells of the Rees. The trail heads across the forested slope of Craigairie Fell, then descends along a good track past Loch Derry to reach the isolated farm of Derry; isolated, but not lacking facilities – there are teas, snacks, a basic camp-site and even B & B offered.

Follow the farm track away from Derry, heading through another area of forest. A minor road crosses rivers and passes through a clearing, then another road leads to Knowe. The trail leads through another patch of forest, then follows a road past Glenruther. The route crosses the low hill of Glenvernoch Fell, then rejoins the road. At Garchew, cut across fields to descend to Bargrennan, which has a hotel, B & B and a small camp-site.

Bargrennan to Dalry

24 miles (39km)

This is a long, hard day's walk, with no B & B accommodation available in between. There is, however, a camp-site with a small shop in Glen Trool, a remote bothy at White Laggan and a bunk-house at Mid Garrary. That represents the full range of facilities for the day. The Southern Upland Way leaves Bargrennan and climbs over the low, forested Rig of the Cairn. The Water of Trool is followed fairly closely to Caldons camp-site – a way which can be wet and boggy. There is a small shop at the camp-site and it's your last opportunity to buy supplies before Dalry.

The trail passes through the Galloway Forest Park on clear paths and tracks. The path leaving Caldons is rocky and muddy in places. When the English army came this way in 1307, Robert the Bruce and his army trundled boulders onto them from the steep slopes above. Eventually, the path becomes easier and a good track climbs above Glenhead Burn. There are fine views across to Loch Dee and the Rhinns of Kells. There's also a bothy at White Laggan offering simple shelter and a log fire.

Cross the Black Water of Dee and continue along broad forest tracks to Clatteringshaws Loch. Tracks and paths lead out of the forest near the Mid Garrary bunk-house and cross Shield Rig before descending to a road alongside Garroch Burn. There is a Southern Upland Way Vehicle Support based at a B & B in Dalry, which can meet you at this road end by prior arrangement. It's a fairly easy walk to Dalry, but it can seem difficult when you're tired. Follow the road parallel to Garroch Burn, then walk over the end of Waterside Hill. Dalry lies across the Water of Ken and has a splendid range of facilities for such a small village.

Dalry to Sanquhar

27 miles (43km)

This is the longest day's walk in the book, but there are ways of shortening it. If you're taking advantage of the Southern Upland Way Vehicle Support, then you can break your journey at Stroanpatrick and be brought back to Dalry for another night. In the morning you'd continue the walk from Stroanpatrick to Sanquhar. The only other accommodation options along this stretch are: Kendoon Youth Hostel (off-route); B & Bs at Murdochwood and Dalquhairn (both off-route); or the Chalk Memorial Bothy (on-route near Polskeoch). Backpackers have plenty of scope for pitching discreetly in the wilds.

Paths and tracks leave Dalry to pass Ardoch and cross Earlstoun Burn. A short road walk leads to Butterhole Bridge, where a detour heads downstream to Kendoon Youth Hostel if required. Crossing Culmark Hill, there are good views ahead of the bulky Cairnsmore of

Carsphairn, then a road is crossed at Stroanpatrick. The trail crosses the newly forested Manquhill Hill, then climbs to the 580m summit of Benbrack. Keep an eye on your map and guide in poor weather for the walk along the crest of these hills.

Stay near the forest to get round to Black Hill, then enter a forest to reach the Covenanter memorial at Allan's Cairn. A lengthy descent through the forest leads to the Chalk Memorial Bothy near Polskeoch. A flush toilet in this remote place is a luxury! If you're not staying at the bothy, then follow a road down the glen. After passing remote farms, the trail leaves the road at the farm of Polgown. A path climbs gently above the glen, crosses Cloud Hill, then descends gently towards Sanquhar. The town should be able to supply everything you need. It also has a museum and the oldest post office in Britain.

Sanquhar to Wanlockhead

8 miles (13km)

This short day's walk can either be used to aid recovery after the previous day's long trek, or it can be added to a half day walk if you've reached Sanquhar from the Chalk Memorial Bothy. It's a hilly walk and ends with a splendid mining site which needs time to explore properly.

A gentle climb over a low, broad hill leads away from Sanquhar, then a steeper climb leads into the hills beyond. There's a choice of routes when you've descended to forests at Cogshead. One route follows forest tracks and paths around the heads of small burns and crosses the spurs of hills. This route is available throughout

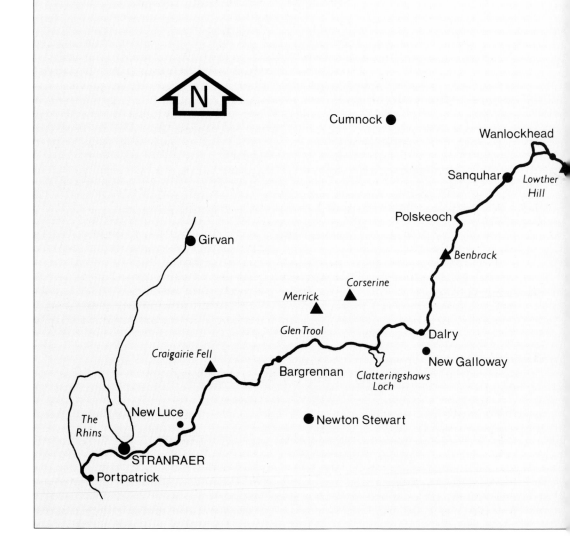

SOUTHERN UPLAND WAY

GLASGOW

Cumnock

Wanlockhead

Sanquhar　Lowther Hill

Polskeoch

Girvan

Benbrack

Corserine

Merrick

Glen Trool

Dalry

Craigairie Fell

New Galloway

Bargrennan　Clatteringshaws Loch

The Rhins

New Luce

Newton Stewart

STRANRAER

Portpatrick

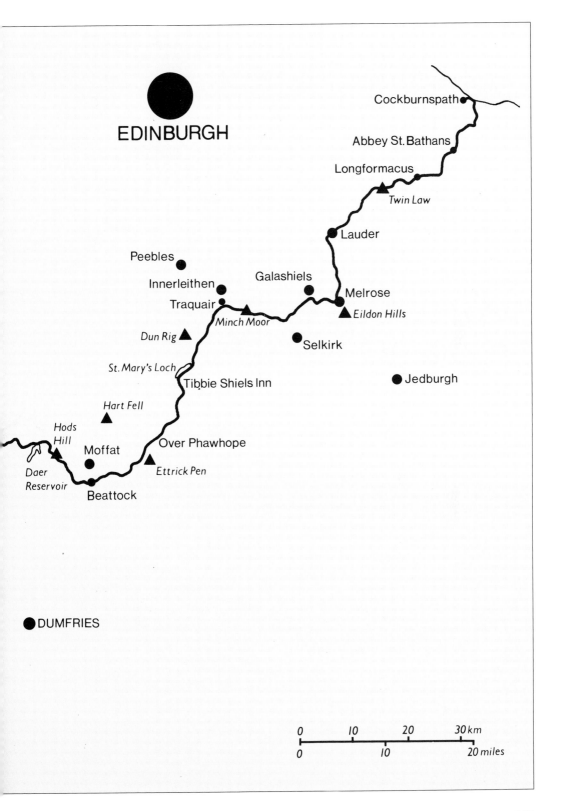

the year. The other route is much shorter and simply heads straight across Glengaber Hill, almost reaching 500m. However, walkers are asked not to use this route between April and the beginning of June, or mid-August to the beginning of November. These restrictions are to accommodate lambing time and grouse shooting.

Whichever way you reach Wanlockhead, be sure to spend time studying what amounts to an immense open-air mining museum. It will cost you some extra distance too. The village, which claims to be the highest in Scotland, has a youth hostel, camp-site, B & Bs, shop and pub.

Wanlockhead to Beattock

20 miles (32km)

Leave Wanlockhead to climb to the highest point on the Southern Upland Way – 725m on Lowther Hill. You'll find a road also zigzags to the summit to serve radomes and masts. Walk down the other side of the hill, noting the extensive views across the Southern Uplands. Fences and walls lead across Cold Moss, Comb Head and Laght Hill before the descent finally leads to a road at Over Fingland. After crossing Potrail Water a forest track is used to reach a road near Daer Reservoir.

Climb up Sweetshaw Brae to reach Hods Hill. The trail goes along a half forested, half moorland crest. The descent from the crest is on the forested side and finally crosses a small river. Just upstream is the bothy of Brattleburn, if shelter is required. The route continues over Craig Hill, then crosses pasture to reach Garpol Water. Another forested stretch leads over Neath Hill, then a road walk heads down to Beattock. There is B & B accommodation and a camp-site in the village. It's also a good idea to do some shopping as supplies could be difficult to obtain for the next couple of days.

Beattock to Tibbie Shiels Inn

21 miles (34km)

The trail leaves Beattock and crosses Annandale. There is a low hill on the way, but you'll have to go round it from mid-March to mid-May to avoid disturbance at lambing time. After a walk alongside Moffat Water there's a track following Cornal Burn high into a large forest. When the trail reaches the top end of the forest there's an attractively rugged gap between the hills and at Ettrick Head the altitude is about 530m.

A forest track leads down to a bothy at Over Phawhope. This could provide useful shelter for visitors struggling along the way in bad weather. It was obviously once a fine farm-stead. There's a long road walk down the Ettrick Valley. Farms are quite widely spaced, but further along you'll be able to call on odd ones to provide B & B, a basic camp-site or snacks. At Scabcleuch there's a climb back into the hills alongside Scabcleuch Burn. The route touches 450m at a gap in the hills, then crosses a valley at Riskinhope Hope. From a forest on Earl's Hill, a good track leads down to Tibbie Shiels Inn. You can get food, drink and lodgings at the inn, or camp alongside. There's also a cafe by the Loch of the Lowes and close to that is a statue of the poet James Hogg, known as the 'Ettrick Shepherd'.

An old beam engine and mine cottages are preserved at Wanlockhead

James Hogg 'The Ettrick Shepherd' overlooks the Loch of the Lowes

Tibbie Shiels Inn to Broadmeadows

22 miles (35km)

A path and forest track lead along the shore of St Mary's Loch, then the trail heads for the hills via Dryhope and Blackhouse. The route touches 476m on the shoulder of Deuchar Law and 461m on Blake Muir. After that, a lengthy descent leads to a road at Kirkhope. This road has to be followed to Traquair, or all the way to Innerleithen if you need to do any shopping. There are no shops near the route until Galashiels.

A good track leads above Traquair and passes through forests to reach the Cheese Well on Minch Moor. The Southern Upland Way has been routed along an unplanted crest on Hare Law, then reaches 524m on Brown Knowe. The trail uses a fine, old drove road which provides good views in clear weather. At Bovery Law it's time to make a decision about the night's lodgings. Backpackers could camp discreetly on the heights, but anyone looking for B & B would have to continue to Selkirk or Galashiels. Broadmeadows Youth Hostel is easily reached by walking downhill from the moorland crest as directed by a sign.

Broadmeadows to Lauder

21 miles (34km)

Hostellers must climb back into the hills from Broadmeadows, finally reaching 464m at the tall cairns known as the Three Brethren. The descent from the hill soon leads into forests where the trail can be muddy. Emerging at the little village of Yair, cross the River Tweed and follow tracks and paths over Hog Hill towards Galashiels. Shops, pubs and other facilities abound, but the route stays above the town and later descends towards the Tweed again with a view of Abbotsford, once the home of Sir Walter Scott. A walk along an old railway trackbed and riverside paths lead to Melrose. Anyone needing a break at this point will find that the town has a youth hostel, B & Bs, camp-site, shops, pubs, etc. Above the town are the three Eildon Hills. Melrose Abbey is worth some moments of study before leaving.

It's not a difficult walk onwards to Lauder. Cross the suspension footbridge over the River Tweed, then follow clear tracks above Wester and Easter Housebyres. The route is very direct, cutting straight across Mosshouses Moor and including a stretch along a minor road. There's a feeling of height, though the route barely scrapes 300m on Woodheads Hill. A path leads down to Lauder Burn and Lauder is soon reached. There's B & B available, as well as a couple of camp-sites and a range of shops and pubs. Make the most of the shops – the next ones are at the end of the walk.

Lauder to Longformacus

15 miles (24km)

Beyond Lauder, the Southern Upland Way crosses the broad Lammermuir Hills. It's not a place to go wrong in misty weather, as you could be wandering for some time. The day's walk starts easily by crossing Lauder Water, then uses forest and farm tracks to gain height. It's a bit of a switchback route as the trail crosses Snawdon Burn and Blythe Water. After heading over Scoured Rig and passing a small forest a track leads down to a remote building at Braidshawrig.

A good track leads over the moors, gradually climbing towards the higher parts of the Lammermuirs. A path heads across the moors

125

Walkers on the Southern Upland Way approaching Blackhouse

and reaches the two cairns on Twin Law at 447m. One cairn has collapsed, while the other cairn has a niche containing a visitors' book. Most of the signatures in the book belong to Southern Upland Wayfarers. The descent from Twin Law leads down to Watch Water, then a track runs around Watch Water Reservoir. A road continues down to the village of Longformacus. There's only one B & B, so you'll need to book in advance. The next accommodation is at Abbey St Bathans.

Longformacus to Cockburnspath

17 miles (27km)

After following a road away from Longformacus, the Southern Upland Way climbs gently uphill past Moor Plantation and Owl Wood to reach 315m before descending through the recently felled Lodge Wood. The route stays above Ellemford Bridge, but eventually runs down through Roughside Wood to follow Whiteadder Water a short way downstream. Abbey St Bathans is a charming estate village, with facilities limited to a youth hostel and tearoom. It's still a fair stride to Cockburnspath, so think twice before turning down the offer of tea.

There are no great hills to climb, but the Southern Upland Way is forever wandering uphill and downhill in the final stages. It passes the isolated farms of Whiteburn and Blackburn Mill, then visits a group of cottages on a hill top at Blackburn. A road leads down to a very busy road and the trail is sandwiched between a road and railway for a while. After crossing the railway a track leads high across a wooded slope. Coming downhill, a valley leads almost to the sea. Before reaching the sea, head uphill and walk along a short cliff path. This overlooks the tiny Cove Harbour before the Southern Upland Way turns inland to end at Cockburnspath. Although only a small village, there are shops, pubs, B & Bs and small campsites.

SOUTHERN UPLAND WAY INFORMATION

Schedule:	*miles*	*km*
Portpatrick – New Luce BB	23	37
New Luce – Bargrennan BB	17	27
Bargrennan – Dalry BB	24	39
Dalry – Sanquhar BB	27	43
Sanquhar – Wanlockhead YH	8	13
Wanlockhead – Beattock BB	20	32
Beattock – Tibbie Shiels Inn BB	21	34
Tibbie Shiels – Broadmeadows YH	22	35
Broadmeadows – Lauder BB	21	34
Lauder – Longformacus BB	15	24
Longformacus – Cockburnspath BB	17	27
Total distance	215	345

Maps:
OSGB 1:50,000 Landranger Sheets 67, 73, 76, 77, 78, 79 & 82.

Guidebooks:
The Southern Upland Way, Western Section and *Eastern Section*, both by Ken Andrew, published by HMSO. *A Guide to the Southern Upland Way*, by David Williams, published by Constable & Co. Ltd.

Accommodation List:
Scottish Natural Heritage.

Tourist Information Centres:
Stranraer, Sanquhar, Moffat, Galashiels, Melrose, Dunbar.

The West Highland Way (map p.136)

The West Highland Way is a popular route leading from the outskirts of Glasgow to Fort William. It's mostly low level, but threads its way between several quite lofty mountains. It's usually routed along good paths and tracks, but there are some parts which can be quite difficult. Several lengths of an old military road are used to good effect, crossing barren moorlands and passing through lonely glens. The route measures 92 miles (146 km) and takes up to a week to walk.

Accommodation options are varied. There are only a couple of youth hostels, but B & B is available in most places. There are also a number of bunk-houses which offer hostel-type lodgings. If you choose to use these, it might be an idea to carry a sleeping-bag.

Backpacking is also a good way to complete the walk, staying on small, informal sites. Permission can be sought for other pitches. Some of the hotels along the way are typical of those in the remote parts of Scotland, offering food, drink and lodgings to travellers; maybe even serving as post office and basic shop. The rugged, muddy shore of Loch Lomond is more difficult to walk than most folk imagine. If you get stuck there, then note the existence of a couple of handy bothies. Although the route often seems to cross broad, bleak, empty country, it's not usually too far to a road and a quick exit. The route seems to attract walkers who would have been better advised to tackle an easier long-distance walk.

Milngavie to Drymen

12 miles (19km)

The first day's walk is very easy, but it lacks the dramatic scenery experienced during the rest of the walk. Anyone arriving at Milngavie by rail will find a huge notice explaining how to reach the start of the walk in the main shopping street. It's an easy stroll alongside Allander Water and through the woods of Mugdock Country Park. Craigallian Loch and Carbeth Loch are both small, pleas-

ant pools. From the path there's a view of the prominent hump of Dumgoyne. A good length of disused railway trackbed follows. There's an invitation for walkers to visit a nearby whisky distillery and have 'one for the trail'. Continue along the trackbed to Gartness, then a minor road leads to Drymen. The village has a range of facilities, or if you started early in the day you could continue to Balmaha.

Drymen to Rowardennan

14 miles (23km)

The West Highland Way climbs gradually uphill from Drymen and wanders through Garadhban Forest. An enormous ladder stile is used to cross the deer fence surrounding the forest. A reconstructed path crosses the steep slopes of Conic Hill. A detour could easily include the 358m summit and there are magnificent views over the island-studded Loch Lomond. The trail descends to the tiny village of Balmaha, which offers B & B, bunk-house

or camp-site accommodation. It's also your last chance to buy food supplies until Crianlarich, though Rowardennan Youth Hostel has a small shop and wayside hotels could supply meals and drinks.

The path along the shore of Loch Lomond is fairly easy at first, but you'll need to keep an eye on its course as it sometimes moves away from the shore and follows a nearby road. The scenery is charming in good weather. When it rains you'll get very wet as the trees continue to drip long after the rain has ceased. There's a camp-site at Cashel which backpackers should note. The shore walk is followed by a short climb up a hill in Ross Wood. Rowardennan Hotel is soon reached and the youth hostel is a short way beyond. A ferry crosses the narrows of Loch Lomond in summer, offering access to Inverbeg Youth Hostel and the main Lomondside road.

Rowardennan to Crianlarich

19 miles (30km)

A good forest track runs from Rowardennan to Ptarmigan Lodge, then there's a choice of routes. A rugged and often muddy path runs close to the shore of Loch Lomond, while an easier alternative simply continues along the forest track. Both routes meet beyond the Rowchoish Bothy, which offers shelter on this long day's walk. As you forge onwards along these steep, rocky, wooded slopes, squelching through mud and tripping over exposed tree roots, you may feel you're never going to reach the head of Loch Lomond. The Inversnaid Hotel is an unexpected sight, served surreptitiously by road from Glen Arklet and by a summer ferry service across the loch.

The Lomondside path becomes rather more difficult and you'll have to bear this in mind when you make your plans. If you can appreciate your surroundings, then this part is managed as a nature reserve and you might notice some wild goats. If you're struggling, then Doune Bothy is available for shelter. Things get easier beyond the bothy and there's a summer ferry service across the head of the loch which leads to the Ardlui Hotel. Staying on the trail, climb past Cnap Mor and go down to Inverarnan where a short detour can be made to the interesting Inverarnan Hotel.

Continue by following the River Falloch from the head of Loch Lomond. Although the path can be wet in places it's much easier to follow. Enjoy the powerful Falls of Falloch in a rocky gorge. The West Highland Way goes under a railway, crosses a road, then climbs gently uphill to enter a forest. A descent leads straight to Crianlarich. This little village has a youth hostel, B & Bs and a shop.

Crianlarich to Bridge of Orchy

13 miles (21km)

Leave Crianlarich and climb back up into forest. A path runs uphill and offers fine views across Strath Fillan, taking in several high mountains. The path crosses Herive Burn and leaves the forest to cross the main road and River Fillan. Pass an old monastic site and walk through fields. The route is never far from the River Fillan as it wanders across the road and through a forest to reach Tyndrum. There are hotels, B & Bs, a bunk-house and camp-site at Tyndrum, as well as shops and cafes. You'll need to be sure of your accommodation beyond Tyndrum as lodgings are very limited until Kinlochleven.

The trail is never too far from a main road as it climbs uphill from Tyndrum. The West Highland Way, road and railway all squeeze through a narrow gap between Beinn Odhar and Beinn Bheag. On the gradual descent to the farm of Auch, a wide strath opens out, but the surrounding mountains are quite bleak and rugged. An old military road is being followed, which was constructed in the eighteenth century under the authority of General Caulfeild. The broad track stays near the railway, rather than the main road, but all routes converge on Bridge of Orchy. This is only a tiny place, with the hotel providing B & B or bunk-house accommodation, as well as meals and drinks. You could ask permission to pitch a tent.

Loch Lomond – the shore walk can be more difficult than you might imagine

A 'Highland' might be encountered on the way to Bridge of Orchy

Bridge of Orchy to Kinlochleven

20 miles (32km)

A forested climb above Bridge of Orchy touches 370m and allows a fine view of the surrounding mountains. The trail pushes northwards across the Black Mount and Rannoch Moor – an area which seems forbiddingly bleak and remote. It's actually fairly easy to cross. First, there's a descent to the Inveroran Hotel, then a road leads across Victoria Bridge. A fine track starts a gradual climb uphill above a forest. On the way down to Ba Bridge the route is again along the old military road. Views across the moorlands take in a complex series of interconnected lochans. Another gentle climb leads to about 450m, then there's a descent to Blackrock Cottage. Note the ski tows on the mountainside before a road is followed to the Kingshouse Hotel. There is food, drink, bunk-house or B & B accommodation at this point. Think twice before passing by as there's nothing else until Kinlochleven.

The military road stays close to the main road, but there's a parting of the ways at Altnafeadh. The military road climbs steeply uphill, zigzagging on the higher, rockier slopes. This is known as the Devil's Staircase and reaches a gap at about 550m which is the highest point gained on the West Highland Way. The route descends across small burns and gradually runs down to Kinlochleven as a broad track. There are patchy woodlands and small waterfalls, as well as unsightly pipelines carrying water to an aluminium works in town. Despite the grim aspect, Kinlochleven has plenty of facilities, including a bunk-house and nearby camp-site. There's also a visitor centre which explains all about the aluminium industry.

Kinlochleven to Fort William

14 miles (23km)

A wooded, rugged path zigzags above Kinlochleven and joins a good track leading into a high glen. This is the old military road again, and the surrounding scenery is

splendid. The trail reaches 330m in the glen and passes ruined buildings at Tigh-na-sleubhaich and Lairigmor. After turning around a rocky corner, the track runs straight through a forest and almost lands on a road at Blar a'Chaorainn. At that point, the West Highland Way heads up into a forest and across the hillside. Eventually, the rugged and forested slopes overlooking Glen Nevis are reached. The huge bulk of Ben Nevis dominates the scene. There are all sorts of ways to end the walk, depending on the time and your choice of accommodation. Either head for Fort William and its excellent range of services, or stay in Glen Nevis and avail yourself of the youth hostel or camp-site; or wander up to Achintee for a night at the bunk-house. Achintee is at the start of the walk up Ben Nevis, if you've any surplus energy to burn off in the morning.

(*overleaf*) **Tigh-na-sleubhaich and Stob Ban high above Kinlochleven**

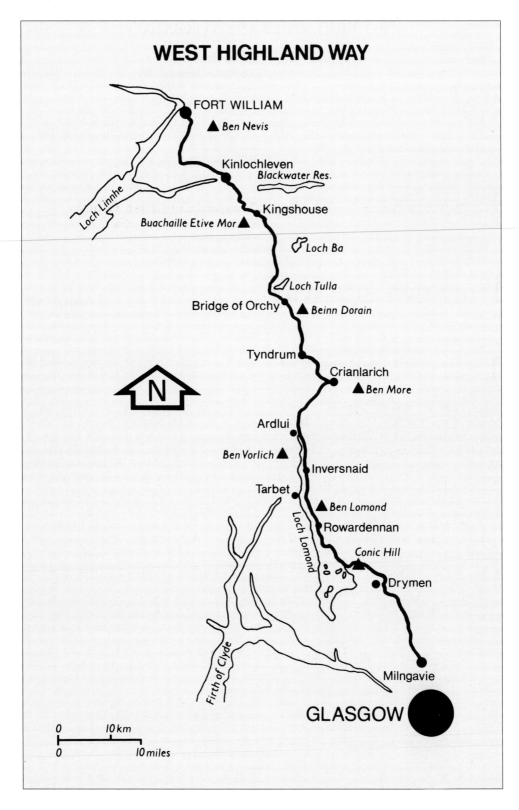

WEST HIGHLAND WAY INFORMATION

Schedule:

	miles	*km*
Milngavie–Drymen BB	12	19
Drymen–Rowardennan YH	14	23
Rowardennan–Crianlarich YH	19	30
Crianlarich–Bridge of Orchy IH	13	21
Bridge of Orchy–Kinlochleven IH	20	32
Kinlochleven–Fort William YH	14	23
Total distance	92	148

Maps:

OSGB 1:50,000 Landranger Sheets 41, 50, 56, 57 & 64.

Guidebooks:

The West Highland Way, by Robert Aitken, published by HMSO. *The West Highland Way*, combined map/guide published by Footprint. *A Guide to the West Highland Way*, by Tom Hunter, published by Constable & Co. Ltd.

Accommodation List:

Scottish Natural Heritage.

Tourist Information Centres:

Glasgow, Drymen, Tyndrum, Kinlochleven, Fort William.

The Speyside Way

(map p.139)

This is a fairly short and easy route, with the focus much more on natural history and heritage than on any sense of challenge. Originally, the Speyside Way was supposed to follow the River Spey from Spey Bay to Nethy Bridge, before wandering through forests to Glen More Forest Park, near Aviemore. Plans have had to be altered radically and the inland terminus is now at Tomintoul on the fringe of the Cairngorms. There's a possibility that the seaward end will ultimately be extended along the coast to Banff.

This is an ideal route for novices to tackle and it's much easier than the other Scottish routes. Starting with riverside paths around Fochabers, there are later stretches of minor roads and forest tracks. Level railway trackbeds keep the central portion close to the River Spey, then low, heather-covered hills are crossed to reach Tomintoul. There are benches and picnic sites along the way for weary walkers, plus a range of visitor centres dealing with subjects as diverse as fishing, soup and whisky. There are opportunities to sample the odd free tot of whisky, for which Speyside is famous.

Accommodation is plentiful, ranging from informal camp-sites to hostels and B & Bs. During the summer months there's a bus called the Speyside Rambler which serves most parts of the trail. There's no doubt that the Speyside Way has an impressive range of facilities. Depending on how you treat the spur to Dufftown, the route could measure from 50 miles (80km) to 60 miles (96km). It should take only three or four days to complete the route.

Spey Bay to Dufftown

22 miles (35km)

Accommodation at Spey Bay is limited to a camp-site and hotel. If you're starting early in the day, you may be able to walk to Craigellachie or Dufftown, but if you're starting in the afternoon it would be better if you spent your first night at Fochabers. There's a visitor centre at Tugnet, on Spey Bay, devoted largely to the salmon fishing industry. Large shingle banks mark the confluence of the powerful River Spey with the moody North Sea. Riverside paths and tracks lead upstream, then woods screen off a view of the river. Later,

A view along the snaky Spey from the forested slopes of Ben Aigen

when the riverside is regained, flooding can be a problem on adjacent tracks. At Fochabers you could break for food and drink, or seek B & B or camp-site accommodation. There's a museum in town and a visitor centre at Baxter's. They call Speyside 'The Larder of Scotland' and Baxter's make a fine range of soups and jams. There are waymarked walks from the factory and a good view is available along the river to Spey Bay.

A fiddly path leaves Fochabers and climbs to a minor road. The road stays away from the River Spey, but you could include a visit to a good viewpoint over it at Ordiequish. After some time, the road goes down to the river at Boat o'Brig, where road and rail bridges cross. Follow a farm track past Bridgeton, then go along a forest track to pass a small firing range. The track continues around the forested slopes of Ben Aigan, with occasional views over Strathspey. After a descent from the forest, a minor road runs past Arndilly House to reach the Fiddichside Inn and Craigellachie. A small cottage here has exhibits relating to the Speyside

Way. There's also space for tents, with B & Bs and shops in the village.

A spur from the main route leads to Dufftown. This is routed along an old railway trackbed which curves through the mixed woodlands by the River Fiddich. Dufftown is entered by road and the town has lodgings, shops and a museum. There's also the Glenfiddich distillery, which has a visitor centre and offers free samples.

Dufftown to Ballindalloch

22 miles (35km)

You can either follow the Dufftown spur back to Craigellachie, or save a bit of walking and catch a bus there instead. Either way, you're back at Craigellachie to continue the walk. The trackbed of the former Strathspey Railway is followed throughout the day. This means that the walking is always on good, firm, level surfaces. There is a short walk through a tunnel after leaving Craigellachie, then a range of services can be found at Aberlour. Old station sites are a feature of the walk and there's a good one preserved near a distillery at Carron. The old station at Tamdhu is used as a visitor centre and when you've toured the Tamdhu distillery you'll be offered another free tot of whisky. The Speyside Way follows more curves of the old railway and passes wooded stretches of riverside to reach Blacksboat Station. Tents can be pitched here, or you can continue a little further to Ballindalloch, where the old station has been converted into an independent hostel. There's also B & B accommodation available nearby. This is as much of the old railway as can be followed, and it's the last you'll see of the River Spey.

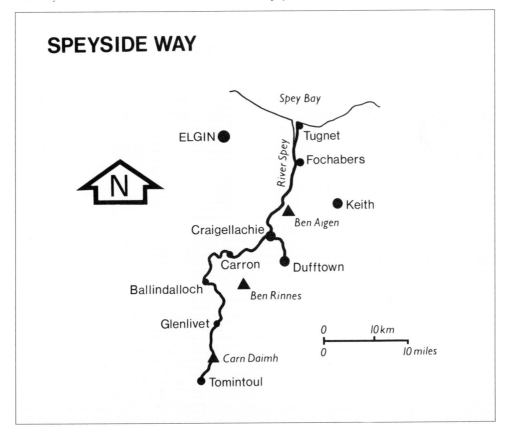

SPEYSIDE WAY

Spey Bay

ELGIN

River Spey

Tugnet

Fochabers

Keith

Ben Aigen

Craigellachie

Carron Dufftown

Ballindalloch

Ben Rinnes

Glenlivet

Carn Daimh

Tomintoul

0   10 km

0   10 miles

Ballindalloch to Tomintoul

16 miles (26km)

Most of the day's walk lies across the Glenlivet Crown Estate. A road walk leads from Ballindalloch and passes a shop near the Old Bridge of Avon. This is guarded by a building with the appearance of a fairytale castle. The Delnashaugh Inn could be visited before farm tracks lead towards the hills. Paths later take the route as high as 460m on hills which are partly heathery and partly forested. There's a good view towards Ben Rinnes before a descent is made from the Hill of Deskie. Cross the River Livet in Glenlivet and follow the trail up through a distillery. There's one last chance for a site visit and free dram.

Deer culling can affect the final part of the Speyside Way and walkers are asked to complete their trip before dusk. A track and clear path lead up onto heathery slopes, finally gaining the stony summit of Carn Daimh. This is the highest part of the trail at 589m. Views look ahead to the bleak Cairngorm plateau, which may be streaked with snow even quite late into the year. A series of downhill stretches remain – through a small forest, across a moor, a bit more forest, then down to a road. There's only Conglass Water to cross, then the walk leads at last to Tomintoul. This is one of the highest villages in Scotland and boasts a youth hostel, bunk-house, B & Bs, shops, pubs and a small museum.

SPEYSIDE WAY INFORMATION

Schedule:

	miles	*km*
Spey Bay – Dufftown BB	22	35
Dufftown – Ballindalloch IH	22	35
Ballindalloch – Tomintoul YH	16	26
Total distance	60	96

Maps:
OSGB 1:50,000 Landranger Sheets 28 & 36.

Guidebooks:
Speyside Way leaflets, published by Moray District Council.

Accommodation List:
Moray District Council.

Tourist Information Centres:
Elgin, Dufftown, Tomintoul.

Ireland

◆

The Wicklow Way

(map p.146)

The Wicklow Way was the first long-distance walking route to be established in Ireland and it remains a challenging upland trail. It starts on the fringes of Dublin and strives to keep high as it crosses the Wicklow Mountains. There are several stretches of broad and boggy moorlands, reaching above 500m in places, as well as some lengthy walks on forest tracks or minor roads. A national park is being established in the area and this should eventually cover most of the high ground. The core areas of the Wicklow Mountains National Park are Powerscourt and Glendalough – popular places which are found on the Wicklow Way.

Youth hostels can be used for the first half of the walk, but B & B accommodation would need to be found later. Backpackers would need to seek permission for pitches, as there aren't any organised sites. The trail measures 82 miles (131km) and the only shops actually on the route occur at Laragh, so detours might have to be made for supplies. The Wicklow Way was originally intended to end at the little village of Moyne, but was later extended to Clonegal so that it could link easily with the South Leinster Way.

There are several guidebooks which claim to cover the Wicklow Way, but they only deal with the northern half of the route. You'll need to be a good navigator on upland stretches in poor weather, and should also take care at junctions of forest tracks. The walk should take under a week to complete. Many walkers choose the Wicklow Way as their first long-distance trail, but fail to complete it as their skills and ability aren't equal to the challenge. There are easier trails more suited for novice walkers.

Marlay Park to Knockree

14 miles (22km)

Frequent buses leave the centre of Dublin for Marlay Park, but the park gates don't open until 10am. Don't get there too early as it would be a pity to miss such a lovely start. It's an easy stroll through the park, with a cafe in the courtyard of a large house, gardens and interesting woodlands, with some sports fields near the exit. A road walk and zigzag forest tracks lead uphill and the boggy slopes of Two Rock Mountain are crossed at about 450m. A rugged slope leads down to a road which runs through Glencullen. Follow this road until there's a way across Glencullen River, though if you went a little further you could break at a handy pub.

Farm and forest tracks climb above Glencullen and there's a short moorland walk around Glencullen Mountain which almost touches 500m. A zigzag descent leads through a forest to a road, then the trail goes round a hill called Knockree. When another road is reached, this can be followed a short way to Knockree Youth Hostel. The hostel was once a farm.

Knockree to Laragh

18 miles (29km)

The Glencree River once had a footbridge, but it was swept away. If it hasn't been replaced, then you could find a way across on a rickety log-jam to save getting wet feet. Forest tracks lead uphill, later there's a splendid view from the top of a rugged, wooded slope. The Powerscourt Waterfall is well displayed as it slides down steep slabs of granite. The Great Sugarloaf is a prominent feature – a hill which is in view from many parts of the Wicklow Way.

The Great Sugarloaf – a hill which is often in view from the forested Wicklow Way

Leave the forest and cross the River Dargle.

There's a stretch across a broad moorland slope and a detour could be made to include the 725m summit of Djouce Mountain. The Wicklow Way only crosses the slopes of Djouce and settles for the 630m summit of White Hill. Views take in the rugged Wicklow Mountains as well as the coast. In optimum conditions it might be possible to see Wales. The descent from White Hill can be boggy, and leads to a fine viewpoint overlooking lovely Lough Tay.

Forest tracks and paths lead over Sleamaine to Lake Park, near Lough Dan. A road walk is followed by paths and tracks leading over Paddock Hill. A descent into woods emerges suddenly at Laragh. There are shops, pubs and tearooms, as well as hostel or B & B accommodation. It's highly recommended that some time be spent exploring nearby Glendalough – a whole day if necessary. The area has lake scenery, forests, nature trails, and the ruins of the Seven Churches which were part of an early monastic site associated with St Kevin. A visitor centre explains all about the place and a visit is recommended.

Laragh to Aghavannagh

18 miles (29km)

Forest tracks climb uphill and stay above Glendalough. Keep an eye on your map and guide, as there are many junctions in the forest and a wrong turning could take some time to sort out. Each track gradually climbs higher, then a final steep ascent leads to the broad, boggy, moorland summit of Mullacor. At 657m, this is the highest point gained by the Wicklow Way. Views in all directions are desolate and the immense bulk of Lugnaquillia rises across Glenmalure.

The trail descends towards Glenmalure, following a series of forest tracks across the steep valley sides. There is a youth hostel in the glen which is available during the summer and at weekends during other seasons. The Wicklow Way reaches a road near Drumgoff Bridge and there's a pub nearby if a thirst needs quenching. Crossing Drumgoff Bridge, note the huge ruined military barracks, which were built in conjunction with a military road through the Wicklow Mountains after the 1798 Rebellion. The trail avoids the military road, which is under tarmac, and uses forest tracks to cross the road at a higher level. The trail twists and turns, finally dropping down to a picnic site by an iron bridge. The tiny village of Aghavannagh is nearby. A youth hostel is hidden behind a screen of trees, occupying another huge barracks building. The hostel has a small store of food if you're running out of supplies.

Aghavannagh to Tinahely

14 miles (22km)

The route from Aghavannagh stays close to the Ow River near the iron bridge, but starts to drift away from it later and climbs up the forested slopes of Shielstown Hill. A descent takes the trail down to a minor road between Askanagap and Moyne. Although the hill seems fairly unremarkable, the only avalanche deaths ever recorded in Ireland occurred on its slopes.

The original terminus of the Wicklow Way was at Moyne, but the village isn't even visited now as the route is taken across a river at Sandyford. A narrow road is followed to Ballycumber, then after fording a stream the trail climbs gently to follow a fine green road around the slopes of Garrymore Mountain. There are wide-ranging views across pleasant pastures and low hilly country. There's a short stretch through a forest, then later a descent to cross Derry River. A short detour leads into Tinahely, which has shops, pubs and B & Bs.

Tinahely to Clonegal

18 miles (29km)

A minor road leads away from Tinahely, then a track is followed around the foot of Muskeagh Hill and through a forest. Road walking takes the trail on a zigzag course across country via Mullinacuff, Kilquiggin and Boley. These tiny villages have no facilities for walkers and if anything is needed you'll have to detour into Shillelagh. After following a road steeply uphill from Boley, there's some fiddly route finding on the forested slopes of Stookeen Mountain. The Wicklow Way finally leaves the forest and goes down a broad, clear track to join a road.

There's another forested walk over Moylisha Hill and Urelands Hill. The trail finally runs down to a road and leads across the County Bridge to Clonegal. The village has a shop, pub and B & B accommodation. A fuller range of facilities can be found in neighbouring Bunclody. There's also the option of continuing to Kildavin to walk the South Leinster Way.

The round tower at Glendalough, close to the ruins of the Seven Churches

WICKLOW WAY

BARROW TOWPATH

DUBLIN

Marlay Park

Robertstown

Rathangan

Naas

▲ *Hill of Allen*

Blessington Reservoir

Barrow Line

Djouce Mtn. ▲

Monasterevan

Kildare

Roundwood ●

Vicarstown

WICKLOW MTS. Laragh

Mullacor ▲

ATHY

Lugnaquillia ▲

River Barrow

Maganey

Aghavannagh

N

CARLOW

Garrymore Mtn. ▲

Croghan Mountain ▲

Tullow

Tinahely

Shillelagh

Muine Bheag

Kildavin

Clonegal

● KILKENNY

Bunclody

▲ *Mount Leinster*

River Barrow

Borris

Graiguenamanagh

Brandon Hill ▲

● ENNISCORTHY

Inistioge

St. Mullins

● NEW ROSS

Mullinavat

CARRICK-ON-SUIR **SOUTH LEINSTER WAY**

0   10 km

0   10 miles

WICKLOW WAY INFORMATION

Schedule:

	miles	km
Marlay Park – Knockree YH	14	22
Knockree – Laragh for YH	18	29
Laragh – Aghavannagh YH	18	29
Aghavannagh – Tinahely BB	14	22
Tinahely – Clonegal BB	18	29
Total distance	82	131

Maps:

OSI 1:50,000 Rambler Sheets 50, 56 & 62. Half Inch Sheets 16 & 19.

Guidebooks:

The Complete Wicklow Way, by J B Malone, published by The O'Brien Press. *Irish Long Distance Walks*, by Michael Fewer, published by Gill & Macmillan. *The Wicklow Way Map Guide*, published by East West Mapping.

Accommodation List:

Bord Failte.

Tourist Information Centres:

Dublin, Glendalough.

The South Leinster Way

(map p.146)

The fountain of all wisdom in ancient Ireland was known as Conle's Well and it was found somewhere in the Slieve Bloom Mountains. From it flowed seven secret streams of knowledge, including the 'Three Sisters', or the Rivers Barrow, Nore and Suir. They began to flow on the night Conn of the Hundred Battles was born.

The South Leinster Way includes walks alongside the Barrow, Nore and Suir, while upland stretches cross the slopes of Mount Leinster and Brandon Hill. This is a fairly easy walk from Kildavin to Carrick-on-Suir in the south east of Ireland. The route measures 60 miles (96km) and can be used to boost the length of the Wicklow Way. In its entirety, the South Leinster Way would take only three or four days to walk.

There are no youth hostels or organised camp-sites along this trail, but there are plenty of B & Bs. Every town and almost every village can provide accommodation. It's an ideal walk for novice long-distance walkers and no parts are really difficult. Provided a careful eye is kept open for waymarks, there should be no problem. Eventually, when the enormous Munster Way is open, the Wicklow and South Leinster Ways will be linked to the Beara and Kerry Ways. In effect, there will be a coast to coast route marked across Ireland.

Kildavin to Graiguenamanagh

22 miles (35km)

Kildavin is a quiet little village which has been bypassed by a busy road. It's not far from Clonegal, where the Wicklow Way ends. There are a shop and pub if food and drink are required, then walkers are directed along a narrow farm road which crosses the bypass. Look out for a marker which shows the way up into a forest. Zigzag tracks lead uphill to a broad saddle between Greenoge and Kilbrannish Hill. The trees thin out a little so that there's a view ahead to Mount Leinster. The trail leads to the Corrabut Gap, where a scenic road leads across the broad, steep slopes of Mount Leinster. A series of up-ended slabs known as the Nine Stones stand beside the road on a gap between Mount Leinster and Slievebawn at around 450m. Cars park here, but some drive up the private road to a TV mast on the 794m summit of Mount Leinster. A summit bid is an optional detour you might like to consider. There are extensive views in clear weather.

Minor roads are followed all the way down to Borris, passing many junctions where you should check signposts and waymarks. Borris is a pleasant little town built alongside the grounds of Borris House. This was the seat of the MacMurragh Kavanaghs – a family with many remarkable members. Borris has shops, pubs and B & B accommodation, if you want to break this long day's walk early.

Roads are followed to Ballytiglea Bridge on the River Barrow, where the Barrow Towpath is followed to Graiguenamanagh. The town is reached after passing four locks, Borris, Ballingrane, Clashganna and the double Ballykennan Lock, on the river. The Barrow flows through an attractively wooded valley and sometimes there are steep, rocky slopes. Graiguenamanagh is a fine town well worth exploring, which has been built around an old abbey church. There are plenty of shops, pubs and lodgings.

The Post Office in the little town of Borris

OIFIG AN PHOIST Borris

post

Graiguenamanagh to Mullinavat

25 miles (40km)

A farm road above Graiguenamanagh runs into forest tracks on the slopes of Brandon Hill. Look carefully for waymarks at all junctions of tracks in the forest. You could, if you wish, follow a hill track above the forest to visit the 519m summit of Brandon Hill. This carries a large cross and cairn – noticeable in distant views. The forest tracks eventually lead into a series of farm tracks and fields above the Nore valley. Follow a track down to Kilcross, then continue to Inistioge by road. A final steep descent leads to a bridge across the River Nore. Inistioge has an attractive riverside and a neat central square. There are shops, pubs and lodgings if you want to make this long day's walk into two easier ones.

A riverside path leads downstream to the tidal limits of the Nore, but the trail is a long way from the sea. Various tracks are followed through mixed woodlands which have been planted in the grounds of Woodstock House. The house itself was burnt in the 1920s. The trail wanders up to a minor road, then more forest tracks lead over the ambitiously named Mount Alto. The tracks lead from one forest to another, then you should keep your eye open for waymarks over Carraghmore before the descent to Ballykenna. Minor roads lead through Glenpipe, then a direct line is taken along a track to cross a broad, forested rise. A gentle descent leads to a road, which is followed to Lukeswell. This tiny village has a pub and stands by a busy road. The main road is avoided by taking a track alongside a nearby railway. Eventually, Mullinavat is reached and there are a shop, pub and B & B accommodation to be found in the village.

Mullinavat to Carrick-on-Suir

15 miles (24km)

The final day's walk is routed entirely along minor roads and passes through quiet, unremarkable country. Shortly after leaving Mullinavat, there's a waterfall beside the road which can be viewed. Afterwards, most road junctions are signposted for Piltown and several small farms and forests are passed before the village is gained. There's a busy road to cross and opportunities to buy food and drink. The main road leads to Carrick-on-Suir, but the trail goes along a quiet minor road closer to the River Suir. There's an old graveyard which can be inspected, or a roadside view of Tibberaghy Castle. At Three Bridges the main road has to be used to reach Carrick. The town has a full range of facilities and the banks of the River Suir should be visited. The Munster Way is routed along the river and is destined ultimately to link with the Beara and Kerry Ways.

SOUTH LEINSTER WAY INFORMATION

Schedule:

	miles	km
Kildavin – Graiguenamanagh BB	22	35
Graiguenamanagh – Mullinavat BB	25	40
Mullinavat – Carrick-on-Suir BB	15	24
Total distance	62	99

Maps:
OSI 1:50,000 Rambler Sheets 68 & 75. Half Inch Sheets 19, 22 & 23.

Guidebooks:
Irish Long Distance Walks, by Michael Fewer, published by Gill & Macmillan.

Accommodation List:
Bord Failte.

Tourist Information Centre:
Carrick-on-Suir.

The Barrow Towpath (map p.146)

All the great rivers in Ireland were held, in ancient times, to start from a single, sacred well. Around this grew nine hazel trees, and crimson nuts falling into the well were eaten by the Salmon of Knowledge. No person could approach the well without due care and reverence, or it would erupt in fury and flood the plains. You're spared a visit to that awesome well by picking up the River Barrow halfway along its course at Athy. The River Barrow is navigable and is connected to the Grand Canal by the Barrow Line. The extent of the navigation, from Lowtown on the Grand Canal to the tidal limit of the Barrow at St Mullins, is 70 miles (112km).

It's an easy, low-level route with the grass and weeds being mown along the tow-path

from time to time. The walk should take about four days to complete. There are one or two overgrown parts, and in places the tow-path has gone under tarmac. Most of the towns and villages along the Barrow offer shops, pubs and lodgings. Although there are no real organised camp-sites, backpackers could ask permission to pitch tents along the way. The Inland Waterways Association of Ireland produces guides to the River Barrow and Barrow Line. These are primarily intended for cruisers, but walkers will find that they contain plenty of helpful and interesting information. Once you've walked the tow-path, you might be able to negotiate for a job as a deckhand on a passing cruiser and get a lift back.

Lowtown to Monasterevan

14 miles (22km)

The Grand Canal stretches from Dublin to the River Shannon, while the Barrow Line branches from it at Lowtown. There's a boatyard where cruisers can be hired, and a footbridge spanning the canal has a large sign giving various distances on the way to St Mullins. There are actually two parallel canals you could follow – the Old Barrow Line and the New Barrow Line. These meet near Ballyteague Castle. Views from the raised banks include the local landmark called the Hill of Allen. You'd be largely unaware of the enormous raised bogs

nearby which are worked for fuel, but look for distant cooling towers of turf-fired power stations. You can check your progress with reference to locks and bridges, noting how remarkably consistent the canal architecture is. The stretch being followed to Monasterevan was completed in 1785. Cross Glenaree Bridge and use the tow-path on the eastern bank.

Rathangan is a small town with shops, pubs and limited lodgings – it's worth a visit. You'll also notice the River Slate running parallel to the canal. There's a double lock at Spencer

Bridge on leaving town. Keep to the eastern bank to continue to Monasterevan, where there are large derelict canalside mills. The town is worth exploring and it has shops, pubs and B & B accommodation. The River Barrow is also encountered, but the trail doesn't follow it yet. It's too shallow and weedy for boats, but it was once considered for upgrading to navigable status.

Monasterevan to Athy

14 miles (22km)

There are plenty of canal works to study around Monasterevan. There's an aqueduct across the River Barrow and a branch from the canal once served Mountmellick. The easiest course is found on the eastern bank of the canal, then a stretch of road has to be followed from Fisherstown Bridge to Courtwood Bridge. After crossing Gratton Aqueduct the tow-path reaches Vicarstown. This stretch of the canal, running to Athy, was completed in 1791.

Food and drink can be found at Vicarstown, if a short break is required. The tow-path continuing towards Athy is largely under tarmac, but it's a quiet minor road which should be no great hardship to walk. Cross the Camac Aqueduct and you'll later find that the road is sandwiched between the Barrow Line and the River Barrow. Cross Cardington Bridge and follow a short stretch of tow-path into Athy. You can continue as far as the lock which finally gives access to the River Barrow, then cross the lovely Horse Bridge and walk back into town. There are plenty of shops and pubs, plus a few B & Bs. Athy has a riverside castle and other buildings of note.

Athy to Muine Bheag

21 miles (34km)

Although the River Barrow has been reached at Athy, you won't always be tracing its course exactly. There are several weirs on the river and the tow-path follows a series of short side canals to locks. Leave Athy on the eastern bank of the river and follow a short side canal to Ardreigh Lock. The true riverside is joined later, then there's a longer side canal which runs towards the tiny hamlet of Tankardstown. The tow-path is overgrown for a short stretch, but the road is just alongside in case of any difficulty. Note an interesting lifting bridge and an old mill of considerable character. After a riverside walk to Maganey Bridge a short detour could include the Three Counties pub. The counties referred to meet nearby and are Kildare, Laois and Carlow. When Carlow town is reached it's worth having a look round the museum. A large castle stands by the river and there are shops, pubs and lodgings if anything is required.

Cross Carlow Bridge to follow the tow-path along the western bank of the Barrow. The countryside is quickly regained and the trail soon passes Clogrennan, which has some interesting buildings. The tow-path continues to Millford, where the river breaks into a series of channels. If nettles are a problem, then follow a road and cross a little bridge near a solitary B & B. A lovely stretch of the tow-path continues past islands in the river, then goes under the new Cardinal Moran Bridge. Leighlinbridge is the oldest bridge on the river, dating from 1320. The small town of the same name is charming and you might choose to spend the night there. Cross the old bridge and follow the tow-path on the eastern bank. There are a couple of side canals on the way to Bagenalstown, or Muine Bheag, where there are plenty of shops and pubs, and a few B & Bs available. Plans by Walter Bagenal to build a town of splendid architecture in the eighteenth century never really materialised.

A splendid old mill stands derelict by the river at Tankardstown

Muine Bheag to St Mullins

21 miles (34km)

The River Barrow is followed faithfully from Muine Bheag and any side canals are quite short. There's a rather messy limeworks by the river, but the village of Goresbridge is pleasant and you could break there for food and drink. Continuing downstream, Ballytiglea Bridge is reached and the South Leinster Way also uses the Barrow Towpath to reach Graiguenamanagh. The town is gained after passing four locks, Borris, Ballingrane, Clashganna and the double Ballykennan Lock, on the river. The Barrow flows through an attractively wooded valley and sometimes there are steep, rocky slopes. Graiguenamanagh is a fine town, well worth exploring, which has been built around an old abbey church. There are plenty of shops, pubs and lodgings.

The final stretch of the Barrow Towpath passes three locks in close succession. There's a lovely, wooded stretch beneath Brandon Hill. At the final lock, you'll notice that the tidal limit of the river has been reached, though it's a long way to the sea. The trail leads as far as the little village of St Mullins. There is food and drink available, and limited B & B accommodation. Spend some time exploring the monastic ruins (associated with St Moling), above the river. There's a holy well nearby, while a climb onto a Norman motte offers fine views of the surrounding country.

BARROW TOWPATH INFORMATION

Schedule

	miles	km
Lowtown – Monasterevan BB	14	22
Monasterevan – Athy BB	14	22
Athy – Muine Bheag BB	21	34
Muine Bheag – St Mullins BB	21	34
Total distance	70	112

Maps:

OSI 1:50,000 Rambler Sheets 49, 55, 61 & 68.
Half Inch Sheets 16 & 19.

Guidebooks:

Guide to the Grand Canal of Ireland, published by the Inland Waterways Association of Ireland. *Guide to the Barrow*, published by the Inland Waterways Association of Ireland. *Irish Long Distance Walks*, by Michael Fewer, published by Gill & Macmillan.

Accommodation List:

Bord Failte.

Tourist Information Centres:

Carlow, New Ross.

The Beara Way

(map p.161)

The Beara Way offers walkers a circuit of the mountainous Beara peninsula in the south west of Ireland. It links with the Kerry Way at Kenmare. The route avoids the scenic Ring of Beara road as much as possible and uses old roads, bog roads and mining tracks to visit places such as Lauragh, Eyeries, Allihies, Castletown Bere, Adrigole and Glengarriff. Some of the tracks which have been incorporated into the route cut across steep, rocky slopes, offering fairly safe walking through extremely rugged country. At the time of writing, not all the route had been waymarked, some sections hadn't been fully negotiated. You might find that some parts follow a slightly different course than outlined in the route description.

Accommodation is fairly plentiful, with a couple of handy youth hostels, a handful of independent hostels and several B & Bs. The main circuit measures 90 miles (145km), though a couple of spurs are planned which would increase the distance. However, if you follow the spurs you'll have to retrace your steps to complete the main circuit. There's also a waymarked route on Bere Island. The route description is restricted to the main circuit, which could easily be completed within a week.

You'll quickly realise that the surname O'Sullivan is dominant in the area. The O'Sullivan Bere clan controlled the area from their base at Dunboy Castle. Eventually, after a concerted campaign by both the English and some local enemies of the clan, the O'Sullivans were forced to flee from Beara. About a thousand men, women and children left on Christmas Day in 1602 to walk to Leitrim. Only thirty-four completed the journey. Eventually, long-distance walks will be linked and new trails formed to re-create the bitter march of the O'Sullivan Bere.

Kenmare to Glanmore

20 miles (32km)

The Beara Way leaves the busy little town of Kenmare by crossing a road bridge over the sea inlet known as Kenmare River. The trail climbs above Killaha, rather than using the coast road, and there are fine views across to the mountainous Iveragh peninsula. A minor road is traced alongside the Dromoghty River on the way to Dromoghty House. The trail crosses a broad, rugged, moorland slope above Muckera, with fine views over the Kenmare River. A descent leads to the lovely Cloonlee Loughs, then a break can be enjoyed at Lake House, which is a pub and restaurant by the road.

Roads are followed through Tuosist, which has a small shop. A road climbs uphill to pass through a gap between the hills of Knockatee and Knockanoughanish. There's a splendid view over Kilmakilloge Harbour before the road zigzags down to Lauragh. A pub is found by the roadside before a turning into Glanmore. Accommodation is tight – there's a camp-site at Creveen Lodge and a youth hostel by Glanmore Lake. A couple of B & Bs lie well off-route.

Glanmore to Allihies

25 miles (40km)

After leaving Glanmore, an old road can be followed from Reenakilta. This is a grassy ribbon across a boggy mountainside. The surroundings seem bleak and desolate and the way can be wet and boggy, but the trail isn't far from the main coastal road. After passing some standing stones (locally known as gallauns) the route goes through a gap near Drung Hill and descends to Glashananinnaun Bridge. The coastal road is followed for a while, then a quieter back road is employed to reach the little village of Ardgroom. Food, drink and accommodation are on offer there.

A minor road leads down to Cappul Bridge, then a climb takes the trail up a rocky, boggy hillside. This is difficult, but once on top the geology works in your favour as you can follow easy lines between parallel bands of rock. There's a road to cross on a gap, then the ridge is followed onwards until it dips towards the sea. Old Kilcatherine Church can be visited; there are a few items of antiquity worth studying. Once a road has been followed around Ballycrovane Bay, there's a tall ogham stone to visit.

The next village is Eyeries, which has pubs, shops and a couple of nearby independent hostels. It's also very colourfully painted. If you're finding this a long, hard day's walk, then you might as well break at this point and continue to Allihies the next day. There's a short walk across a hillside before a descent to a narrow road. The road eventually starts to climb uphill and becomes a clear, stony track. The ascent is fairly gentle and the track crosses a gap in the rugged Slieve Miskish Mountains. Sweeping zigzags take the trail down a very steep and rocky slope in complete safety. The ruins of old copper mines and engine houses will be noticed. Cornish labour was employed there in the past. Allihies is the little village in view below. It has shops, pubs and lodgings, despite its small size. Stay on the Beara Way for a little longer to reach Allihies Youth Hostel outside the village.

Allihies to Adrigole

20 miles (32km)

A road leads from Allihies towards a mast on the summit of Knockgaur. You won't be going that far, but use a track across the shoulder of the hill to descend through forest to Knockoura. A minor road leads across the hillside to pass farms, forest and bogland before descending to Castletown Bere. There are a couple of antiquities signposted from the roadside, such as a prominent rath and a stone circle. Castletown is a busy little place with a full range of facilities, if you want to finish the walk early in the day. Across from the harbour is Bere Island, which can be reached by a short ferry if you want to explore it.

The next part of the Beara Way can be difficult and might take longer than you imagine. Basically, the route crosses the southern slopes of Maulin, Knocknagree and Hungry Hill. The trouble is, you have to climb uphill, cross rugged slopes, then come downhill before repeating the process again and again. There are some helpful bog roads, but there is also some rough country to traverse. The last track used on Hungry Hill is splendid, making the ascent of a steep, rocky slope quite easy. The track ends suddenly and there's a steep, boggy descent into a valley before a road leads off to Adrigole. This scattered little village has a shop, pub, independent hostel and nearby B & B accommodation.

The world's tallest ogham stone on the way to the village of Eyeries

Glengarriff to Kenmare

15 miles (25km)

After visiting Glengarriff Forest the Beara Way follows an old road in preference to the main road. This crosses Esk Mountain at nearly 360m, then descends to join a narrow tarmac road at Esk. To return to Kenmare, simply keep to the eastern side of the Sheen River, avoiding the main road which runs along the western side. The minor roads used are quiet and the route passes a few farms. Look out for the cursing stones known as the Rolls of Butter, close to a ruined church. An old track is followed across Lugummera, then it's a case of following the roads again. A turning at a crossroads at Dereenard takes the Beara Way across Sheen Bridge to reach Riversdale and its hotel. Cross the bridge over the Kenmare River to walk back into Kenmare. A full range of services are offered, including a number of independent hostels.

BEARA WAY INFORMATION

Schedule:

	miles	km
Kenmare – Glanmore YH	20	32
Glanmore – Allihies YH	25	40
Allihies – Adrigole IH	20	32
Adrigole – Glengarriff IH	10	16
Glengarriff – Kenmare IH	15	25
Total distance	90	145

Maps:

OSI 1:50,000 Rambler Sheets 78, 84 & 85. Half Inch Sheets 21 & 24.

Guidebooks:

The Beara Way Map Guide, published by Cork Kerry Tourism.

Accommodation List:

Bord Failte.

Tourist Information Centres:

Kenmare, Castletown Bere, Glengarriff.

Adrigole to Glengarriff

10 miles (16km)

A series of minor roads are followed uphill from Adrigole to a ruined church at Massmount, before proceeding to Curraduff. There are a number of gallauns and other ancient remains to note. An old road leads across a boggy slope. Sometimes it's quite clear, but at other times it's almost overwhelmed by bog. It leads through a rocky gap between Sugarloaf Mountain and Gowlbeg Mountain. A descent leads to a forest in the Magannagan Valley.

The old road continues across the valley, climbs over another gap and descends to Glengarriff Forest. The Beara Way may go that way, or it may be routed along the Magannagan Valley to Derryconnery to reach Glengarriff by road. Glengarriff is a popular place with a splendid range of services. As this is only a short day's walk, there may be time to explore the area. There are a number of short waymarked walks, or you could enjoy a boat trip around Glengarriff harbour and visit the Italian Gardens on Garinish Island.

The Rolls of Butter cursing stones by the road on the way to Kenmare

The Kerry Way

The Ring of Kerry is a popular and long established scenic drive in the south west of Ireland. The Kerry Way is the long-distance walker's version. Basically, it's a scenic circuit of the mountainous Iveragh peninsula, starting from Killarney and taking in such places as Glenbeigh, Cahirciveen, Waterville, Sneem and Kenmare. Between these towns and villages it explores rugged glens, mountainsides and moorlands, with occasional coastal stretches. Old roads and newly created paths are linked to make the circuit, which includes the Killarney National Park and Derrynane National Historic Park.

The distance is variable as there are a number of spurs from the main circuit to various towns and villages. If you omit all these detours, you could complete the walk in as little as 100 miles (160km). However, you might be struggling to find accommodation in some places. If you included all the spurs you'd have a greater range of facilities and would end up covering as much as 135 miles (217km). You'll choose the route which suits you best, taking account of your ability and needs.

There are only a couple of youth hostels handy for the Kerry Way, but there are several independent hostels and B & Bs. Backpackers have only odd organised sites, but can usually find a pitch at the independent hostels. It might also be possible to pitch discreetly in the wilds. It will usually take over a week for walkers to complete the Kerry Way, but it all depends on how you organise the route. It's assumed that you'll start from Killarney, which has the fullest range of services. You could, if you wished, enjoy a tour around the Ring of Kerry first, to get a preview of the sort of country you'll be walking through. There aren't many trails where you could do that.

Killarney to the Black Valley

14 miles (22km)

Everyone heads for Killarney, but the town is really quite unremarkable. It's the surrounding countryside which is special. Leave town by road, heading towards Muckross. There's a network of paths around Muckross House in the Killarney National Park, so look carefully for waymarks on the way through. The house serves as a centre for the national park, so you might like to break there and find out all about the area. The grounds are ornamental, with odd glimpses of the celebrated Lakes of Killarney. Jarveys with jaunting cars will pester you to take a ride, but they can't get far along the Kerry Way.

Walk away from Muckross House to reach Torc Waterfalls and climb up steps alongside. The steep slopes are forested, but the trail emerges from it to follow an old track around the back of Torc Mountain. This is known as the Old Kenmare Road and it runs through a wilderness where red deer can be spotted. Look for waymarks whenever the track becomes vague. A descent is made into a valley full of rhododendrons, then a road leads down to Derrycunnihy Church.

A stony track runs through woodlands to emerge in a bogland close to the Upper Lake. This route is closed in winter as white-fronted geese graze by the lake. The path is firm, but it can flood from time to time. It leads to Lord Brandon's Cottage, where you could break for teas and snacks. A track leads across a bridge and a road is followed into the Black Valley. This is a wild place, where facilities are limited to a youth hostel and small shop.

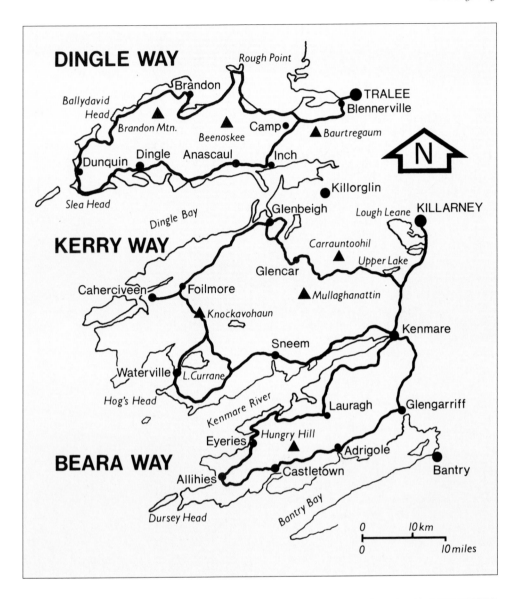

DINGLE WAY

Rough Point

Brandon

Ballydavid
Head

Brandon Mtn.
Beenoskee

Camp

TRALEE
Blennerville

Baurtregaum

N

Dingle Anascaul

Inch

Dunquin

Killorglin

Slea Head

Glenbeigh

Lough Leane KILLARNEY

Dingle Bay

KERRY WAY

Carrauntoohil

Upper Lake

Glencar

Caherciveen

Foilmore

Mullaghanattin

Knockavohaun

Kenmare

Sneem

Waterville L.Currane

Hog's Head

Kenmare River

Lauragh

Glengarriff

Eyeries Hungry Hill

BEARA WAY

Adrigole

Bantry

Allihies Castletown

Dursey Head

Bantry Bay

0   10 km

0   10 miles

The Black Valley to Glenbeigh

20 miles (32km)

Follow the road into the Black Valley, then take a hillside track into a forest. Later, the last stretch of the road in the Black Valley leads to a remote house. A vague route known as the Bridle Path climbs to a rugged gap at nearly 300m between the huge mountains of Broaghnabinnia and Carrauntoohil. A steep and rocky descent into the Bridia Valley reaches a road end. Follow the road a short way down the valley, almost to a solitary B & B.

A track called the Lack Road zigzags up a rugged slope to cross a gap at almost 400m. If you had a day to spare you could climb to Ireland's highest mountain – Carrauntoohil. The Lack Road descends a steep and rocky slope and goes through a wild glen to reach a road near Lough Acoose. Painted signs indicate a nearby B & B and camp-site and there may

161

The Eagles Nest rises above the Upper Lake in the Killarney National Park

one day be a youth hostel in this area. A road walk leads to the Climbers Inn at Glencar, a popular place for walkers with a basic shop and independent hostel. You could end the day's walk here, or continue to Glenbeigh.

A track heads for Bealalaw Bridge, where a short stretch of the River Caragh can be followed. A forest track and stepped path lead to a viewpoint, then there's a descent to a road. The road runs towards a range of hills and after following a track uphill there's a choice of routes. A high-level trail reaching almost 350m crosses a heathery gap in the hills and descends quickly to Glenbeigh. A lower trail contours around the slopes of Seefin at about 200m and finally enters Glenbeigh after a long road walk. Glenbeigh has shops, pubs, B & Bs and a camp-site. There is an interesting 'Bog Village' being developed as an attraction.

Glenbeigh to Cahirciveen

17 miles (27km)

The Kerry Way climbs into a forest over-looking Glenbeigh, then emerges to fol-low the crest of a heather-covered hill rising to 275m. There are good views of the surrounding mountains, as well as those of the Dingle peninsula. A road walk leads to Mountain Stage, then a track continues around the slopes of Drung Hill to enter a forest below Beenmore. A series of old tracks and roads make a beeline for the scattered village of Foilmore. There's a B & B nearby, but the Kerry Way follows an old mass path across the River Ferta. After climb-ing a short way uphill there's a spur leading off to Cahirciveen.

Cahirciveen has a full range of services and is an interesting little town. If you don't go there, you'll have a long and rugged walk before finding alternative accommodation. The way towards the town crosses a broad, barren bogland, but ends with firm tracks and a road walk into town. There's an interesting heritage centre housed in an old barracks.

(*overleaf*) Heading towards the Black Valley
and the lofty MacGillycuddy's Reeks

Cahirciveen to Waterville

19 miles (31km)

Both Cahirciveen and Waterville are on spurs from the Kerry Way, so there's a considerable retracing of steps to be done. First, there's a walk back across the barren bogland to regain the main circuit on the slopes of Coomduff Hill. A walk along the low, rugged moorland crest of the hill has wide-ranging views. After Coomduff Hill, there is another low hill to cross before a descent to a gap. Cross a road near a school on the gap, then head straight uphill again. Fences are useful guides all along this crest, crossing Keelmore Hill and reaching the 376m summit of Knockavohaun. There's no fence leading off towards Canuig Hill, but one appears later and eventually minor roads are followed across a broad, boggy valley.

After crossing the River Inny the trail goes through the tiny village of Mastergeehy to follow an overgrown mass path uphill. Again, there's a choice of routes available, with a spur leading from the main circuit out to Waterville. If you don't want to go to Waterville you'll find a solitary B & B at the foot of the hill. The spur crosses another Coomduff Hill and passes Knag Hill before descending to a road. The road leads into Waterville – a little seaside resort with admirable services. Charlie Chaplin used to spend his holidays here.

Waterville to Caherdaniel

17 miles (27km)

The morning starts with a walk back along the moorland crest to join the main Kerry Way circuit again. You could, of course, take an easier course along a lower road. The trail crosses the Cummeragh River, then joins a road to reach a farm. There's a rugged climb to a shoulder called Mullach Liche, then a descent to a forest at the head of Lough Currane. This lake is in view for much of the day and is seen from all angles. A road leads past Isknagahiny Lough and you might be able to get a pot of tea at the Teach Bride Museum before the next uphill stretch.

There's a steep and rugged climb to the Windy Gap at almost 400m. Views look across to the mountains of the Beara peninsula, then a descent leads across the difficult slopes of Eagles Hill. There's a spur from the Kerry Way to the village of Caherdaniel. Although small, this place has a shop, pub, B & B and independent hostel.

There is a shorter alternative route from Waterville to Caherdaniel, though it may not yet be waymarked. It starts by following minor roads away from Waterville, staying close to Ballinskelligs Bay. Paths and stretches of old roads take the trail close to the Ring of Kerry road and over a rise to a roadside pub. The route continues into a wooded area and a tour of Derrynane National Historic Park could easily be made. This has been created around the home of Daniel O'Connell, known as The Liberator. There's a restaurant on site and an old stone fort can be inspected on the way to Caherdaniel.

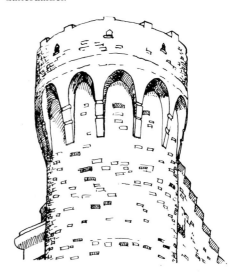

Former police barracks at Cahirciveen – now the local heritage centre

Caherdaniel to Sneem

13 miles (21km)

Again, start the day by retracing steps to return to the main circuit. Follow an old road which later passes a ruined church. Further along, a detour is highly recommended to visit Staigue Stone Fort, whose walls are in a remarkable state of preservation. Back on the Kerry Way, climb up a steep and boggy slope and cross the flanks of some rugged little hills. A messy section leads through a forest, then after a short road walk a series of old roads and tracks are linked to take the trail to Sneem.

Sneem is a neat and attractive little town and a regular 'Tidy Towns' winner. There are two triangular greens on opposite sides of Sneem River, which no doubt inspire a certain rivalry between the two halves of the town to keep their patch the best. There are plenty of services, though the nearest independent hostel is a little further along the trail at Derryquin.

Sneem to Kenmare

19 miles (31km)

Rough tracks, minor roads and a forest track lead from Sneem to Derryquin. A prominent old road can be followed onwards, passing the remains of Old Tahilla Village to reach Tahilla Bridge. There's a shop before you cross the road, then the next part of the trail can be awkward as it leads through a wooded, boggy area. Persevere until you reach the road to cross Blackwater Bridge. A short stretch of coastal walking leads along the shore of Kenmare River – a lengthy sea inlet, despite the name.

Forest tracks lead from Dromore Castle to Cappanacush Castle, then the Ring of Kerry road has to be followed through Templenoe. You can break for food and drink here, but there's no relief from the traffic until the trail is routed back towards the high ground. After climbing to Gortamullin the Kerry Way heads down to Kenmare. This busy little town has plenty of shops, pubs and independent hostels. It's both a colourful and interesting place.

Kenmare to Killarney

16 miles (26km)

A minor road is followed uphill from Kenmare. It runs downhill for a short way, then a track continues uphill to breach a range of rugged hills at nearly 350m on the Windy Gap. A zigzagging track leads down into a wild valley and you'll eventually have to admit that you've been there before. The rhododendrons are a dead giveaway. The Kerry Way is routed uphill, following the Old Kenmare Road back around Torc Mountain. A descent through forest alongside Torc Waterfall returns walkers to Muckross House. There's a chance for another look around the house and grounds before walking back along the road to Killarney. The town has a splendid range of services, being able to supply everything you'll need.

The massive drystone ramparts of the Staigue Stone Fort near Caherdaniel

169

KERRY WAY INFORMATION

Schedule:	*miles*	*km*
Killarney – The Black Valley YH	14	22
The Black Valley – Glenbeigh BB	20	32
Glenbeigh – Cahirciveen IH	17	27
Cahirciveen – Waterville IH	19	31
Waterville – Caherdaniel IH	17	27
Caherdaniel – Sneem IH	13	21
Sneem – Kenmare IH	19	31
Kenmare – Killarney YH	16	26
Total distance	135	217

Maps:
OSI 1:50,000 Rambler Sheets 78, 83 & 84.
Half Inch Sheets 20 & 24.

Guidebooks:
New Irish Walk Guide, Southwest, by Sean O'Suilleabhain, published by Gill & Macmillan. *The Kerry Way Map Guide*, published by Cork Kerry Tourism. *Irish Long Distance Walks*, by Michael Fewer, published by Gill & Macmillan.

Accommodation List:
Bord Failte.

Tourist Information Centres:
Killarney, Glenbeigh, Cahirciveen, Waterville, Sneem, Kenmare.

The Dingle Way

(map p.161)

Dingle – there's a name which rings a bell! It's a small town in Co Kerry, but the name is also used to label a mountainous peninsula. The Dingle Way makes a circuit of the peninsula and takes in stunning scenery and a wealth of archaeological remains. Sometimes the trail runs close to the sea, while at other times it wanders across the slopes of hills and mountains. There's one high pass which needs to be crossed near Brandon Mountain where bad weather could be a particular problem. Advance knowledge of the tide times is useful towards the end of the walk, as there are some lengthy beach walks.

Much of the walking is along clear tracks or minor roads, with hardly any forests. The distance covered is 114 miles (183km) and should take about a week to walk. A knowledge of local legends is handy when you come to study the standing stones, ruined churches and deserted settlements. A trail known as the Saint's Way is also available in the area, linking many ecclesiastical sites and old pilgrimage centres.

Accommodation is plentiful around the Dingle Way. There's only one youth hostel, but several independent hostels and B & Bs are to be found. Food and drink are obtainable from numerous little shops and pubs, or from restaurants in unlikely places. The route description starts from Tralee and covers some distance before the actual circuit of the peninsula begins. It's up to you whether to end the walk by completing the circuit, or by walking all the way back to Tralee. Either way, by the time you've finished the Dingle Way you'll realise why people return to the area time and time again.

Tralee to Inch

17 miles (27km)

Tralee is a busy little town with narrow streets and a full range of services. When you've had a good look around, find the road to Dingle, but don't actually walk along it. The trail follows the tow-path of an old ship-canal linking Tralee and Blennerville. There's a fine windmill at Blennerville and a heritage centre which deals with the causes and effects of emigration from Ireland. Roads lead towards the Slieve Mish Mountains, but the trail doesn't scale the heights. Instead, a path has been constructed across the foot of the range, offering a fairly easy walk over rugged moorlands. There are odd streams to cross and wide ranging views across Tralee Bay. Eventually, an old road is found and this leads through the deserted village of Killelton. There's an opportunity to detour to the village of Camp for food, drink or lodgings.

The old road crosses the Finglas River, then there's a stretch of tarmac road to be followed all the way to Inch. This climbs uphill to cross a gap in the hills, then descends through a boggy valley drained by the Emlagh River. The road runs through a forest before a slight detour leads into Inch. This little village has a shop, pub and accommodation, including an independent hostel. For an evening stroll, wander along Inch Strand.

Inch to Dingle

18 miles (29km)

An old road fringed with fuchsias climbs above Inch and around the slopes of Brickany. After crossing a gap in the hills a road is followed straight down to Anascaul. There are views of the mountains around Lough Anascaul and you could visit a prominent standing stone which is just off the road. Anascaul has a good range of facilities, including a pub called the South Pole which was once owned by Tom Crean, who accompanied Captain Scott on Antarctic expeditions.

Most of the route between Anascaul and Lispole lies along roads, with a scenic interlude at Kilmurry. A beach composed of huge boulders is flanked by cliffs and overlooked by a castle which was once the base of the Knight of Kerry. Lispole has a shop, pub and nearby independent hostel. The Dingle Way leaves Lispole and links a series of farms by using roads, tracks and paths. The line of the route is fiddly, so keep an eye peeled for waymarks. An old road is eventually reached which leads over a rise before descending directly to Dingle. This little town is immensely popular and has a full range of services. There are several independent hostels. Dolphin mania gripped the town after the arrival of Fungi – a wild bottlenose dolphin. He has lived off Dingle Harbour for some years and delights in the boatloads of tourists who go to see him. It's an insecure business for the boatmen, as the dolphin is free to leave at any time without giving notice.

Dingle to Dunquin

14 miles (22km)

As you leave Dingle by road, look out for the standing stones known as the Gates of Glory. The road is succeeded by a hill track, then a descent leads to Ventry. You could break at a nearby restaurant and take on board the history and legends of the area, particularly the Battle of Ventry Strand. This supposedly lasted for a year and a day, with the brave Fianna holding Ireland against the King of the World. The king was ultimately slain and you could later look for his gravestone near Kilvickadownig, after you've walked around Ventry Bay.

There is a road around Slea Head, but the Dingle Way uses higher paths and tracks to make a scenic circuit. Intricate stone walls have been fashioned from rubble cleared off steep slopes. The people who cleared these tiny fields lived in small, drystone beehive huts, which can be seen later. As the trail rounds Slea Head, the Blasket Islands come into view. This is the westernmost part of Europe. Boat trips to the islands can be arranged at Dunquin Pier and these rugged, sea-washed places may become designated a national park. Dunquin is a scattered settlement with a shop, pub, cafe and youth hostel – all looking out to the Atlantic Ocean.

Dunquin to Ballydavid

13 miles (21km)

A track leads from the youth hostel at Dunquin, over a moorland rise to Clogher. A stretch of the shattered coast is followed, then there's a detour around the Dun an Oir Hotel complex. The Dingle Way crosses the land behind the Three Sisters headland and reaches the interesting promontory fort of Dun an Oir. An invasion fleet from Spain landed here in 1580, but was beaten by English forces. The leaders of the fleet were beheaded and a memorial erected on the site recalls the act.

Continue walking around the broad sweep of Smerwick Harbour, mostly walking along the strand. A short detour inland is recommended to visit the remarkable stone chapel called the Gallarus Oratory. There is a campsite and independent hostel nearby. Back on the trail, the Dingle Way leads towards Ballydavid. The name causes some confusion – there was once a coastguard station at Ballydavid, which moved to Ballynagall. The name went with it, so there are two Ballydavids. Perhaps it's best to stick with the original Irish names, particularly as you're now in the heart of the Chorcha Dhuibhne *gaeltacht*, or Irish speaking area. A tall mast nearby is a *Radio na Gaeltachta* transmitter. There are plenty of lodgings available, including an independent hostel.

Ballydavid to Cloghane

18 miles (29km)

Check the weather before starting this day's walk, as there's a climb across a high pass and a walk through some desolate country. It's nearly always damp and misty, as huge mountains rise straight from the ocean, but in foul weather it might be best to hold back for a while. The start of the walk is easy enough, simply following the road to Tiduff. You could detour to Brandon Creek, where St Brendan commenced his remarkable voyage to weird and wonderful islands (some say he reached America). A track above Tiduff is followed by a boggy moorland, then a fairly good grassy ribbon runs plainly uphill. This is an old track built to service a signal station sited on a high gap. Ever present mists meant that signals were hardly ever seen, and the station fell into ruins.

The gap between Masatiompan and Brandon Mountain is over 650m, so this is the highest point reached by any trail in Ireland. There's an ogham stone near the rubble which was once the signal station.

Look carefully for waymarks on the long descent, which has some rather muddy patches. There's a track reached at a place called Arraglen, where farmers once lived and worked. You could detour to overlook Sauce Creek – a cliff-fringed bay where people also farmed the rugged slopes. The Dingle Way leads down a fine, broad track, then takes a circuitous course around Brandon village. There's food and drink on offer before a walk, largely along roads, leads to Cloghane. This little village has a few lodgings.

Cloghane to Castlegregory

18 miles (29km)

Follow roads from Cloghane to Fermoyle, then head for the beach on the broad sweep of Brandon Bay. Stay on the beach for most of the day's walk, which could be difficult if a high tide pushes you onto soft sand dunes. Progress can be measured by keeping an eye on the rugged end of the peninsula. Come ashore at Fahamore and have a look at a ruined church. Nearby facilities are limited to food and drink only. The trail stays on dry land between Fahamore and Kilshannig, with views out to a series of small islands called the Magharees, or Seven Hogs. The trail leads back onto the beach to continue to Castlegregory. This is a more sheltered side of the long, sandy peninsula, but there are pebbly areas to cross. Come ashore at the Trench Bridge and follow a road into Castlegregory. There are shops, pubs and B & Bs in this little village, with an independent hostel nearby at Stradbally.

(*overleaf*) **Brandon Peak is in view, mist permitting, from many parts of the Dingle Way**

Castlegregory to Tralee

16 miles (26km)

Follow a road away from Castlegregory, but almost as soon as you reach the sea you'll have to step inland to Aughacasla. A road leads down to the beach and you follow the beach all the way around Carrigagharoe Point. The trail comes ashore at Killelton. On the first day's walk, Killelton's deserted village was visited, so you can decide whether to end there, or to retrace your steps back across the foot of the Slieve Mish Mountains to reach Blennerville and Tralee.

DINGLE WAY INFORMATION

Schedule:	*miles*	*km*
Tralee – Inch IH	17	27
Inch – Dingle IH	18	29
Dingle – Dunquin YH	14	22
Dunquin – Ballydavid IH	13	21
Ballydavid – Cloghane BB	18	29
Cloghane – Castlegregory BB	18	29
Castlegregory – Tralee IH	16	26
Total distance	114	183

Maps:
OSI 1:50,000 Rambler Sheets 70 & 71.

Guidebooks:
New Irish Walk Guide, Southwest, by Sean O'Suilleabhain, published by Gill & Macmillan. *The Dingle Way and Saint's Road*, by Maurice Sheehy, published by the author. *The Dingle Way Map Guide*, published by Cork Kerry Tourism. *Irish Long Distance Walks*, by Michael Fewer, published by Gill & Macmillan.

Accommodation List:
Bord Failte.

Tourist Information Centres:
Tralee, Dingle.

The Western Way

(map p.183)

The Western Way wanders through mountainous country in the west of Ireland. The scenery is remarkably varied and often dominated by huge, rugged mountains. Old roads and forest tracks are used, but there are also some parts without a trodden path. The route generally keeps to a low level, though there are a couple of high passes. The latter part of the walk is largely along roads with occasional views of the coast.

The Western Way starts in the beautiful Connemara and passes the Maum Turk Mountains and the long inlet of Killary Harbour. At the end of one long day's walk the route runs along the foot of Croagh Patrick – Ireland's holy mountain. You might feel drawn to make an ascent of it. After passing the towns of Westport and Newport, forest tracks lead past the bleak, barren Nephin Beg Range. An area of bogland and forest is followed by occasional coastal walks as the trail passes Ballycastle, Killala and Ballina. Beyond Ballina, the route climbs into the Ox Mountains and ends on a high gap.

The 155 mile (249km) route would take over a week to complete. For the most part, hostels and B & Bs are easily linked on foot, but there are lengthy stretches without accommodation and you might have to move off-route. Backpackers, on the other hand, should have no difficulty obtaining permission for pitches. The route description outlines your options on awkward sections.

Oughterard to Maum

15 miles (24km)

Oughterard is a natural gateway to the charming Connemara and it seems to have everything to please the passing tourist. A range of shops, pubs and lodgings are offered. The Western Way starts by following a road, but not the one heading directly for the shore of Lough Corrib. Instead, a higher road is used at first, which allows a good view over the island-studded lake. Although the shore road is a dead end for motorists, it can be busy as it leads to the lovely Doon Hill viewpoint. Doon Hill is quite small, but it is covered in trees and seems larger than life as it towers over a narrow part of Lough Corrib.

A track leads away from the last farms, then goes through a forest to reach a broad, boggy slope. It takes some time to progress towards the rugged hill of Lackavra, whose steep slopes fall into the water. A ruined mill is passed on the way. Look out for a solitary, abandoned house in a patch of trees on Lackavra. Climb just above the trees to avoid an impasse where a cliff falls into the water. There are also grand views back along the lake and you'll be able to study the ruined Castlekirk on its tiny island. After descending to the shore again, a bog road is joined and this leads towards the scattered village of Maum. There are a shop, pub and a few B & Bs in the valley, which is surrounded by high mountains.

(*overleaf*) **A bog road runs towards the scattered village of Maum**

Maum to Leenaun

20 miles (32km)

A road walk leads from Maum, then after crossing the Failmore River an old pilgrim path is followed onto a gap in the Maum Turk Mountains at Maumeen at almost 260m. The pilgrimage was originally based on St Patrick's Bed and Holy Well, but now features a small chapel and Stations of the Cross. There is a clear track down from Maumeen to the broad, boggy Inagh Valley. A narrow road leads past a few farms and a small church, with views of the rocky Maum Turk Mountains and Twelve Bens of Connemara.

An old road – a ribbon of grass through a bog – is taken across the lower slopes of the mountains. Think twice before following it, because it will take longer to walk than you might think. If you are running out of time, then accommodation can be found well off-route at Kylemore. There are several streams to cross, which can be awkward when they are swollen after heavy rain. A forest track provides a firmer surface for a while, then it's back to the boggy old road and all its streams. Killary Harbour appears below – a long fjord hemmed in by high mountains. Mweelrea is the highest mountain in the Province of Connacht and it rises from the waters of Killary Harbour. The old road eventually runs down to the main coastal road and this is followed into Leenaun. This little village has shops, pubs and B & Bs, as well as a heritage centre dealing with sheep farming and the wool industry. If you have any time and energy to spare, you could continue to Aasleagh or Glenacally Bridge in search of a B & B for the night.

Leenaun to Westport

25 miles (40km)

This is a long, hard day's walk, and the only way to shorten it is to use B & Bs on the road walks at the beginning and end of this stretch. There are a couple of B & Bs around Aasleagh, plus a waterfall which is worthy of a detour. Rugged slopes rising from the road lead to the strangely named Devilsmother. Glenacally Bridge is your last chance to avail yourself of B & B before Westport.

A track leaves the road and crosses the Erriff River before climbing over a rise to reach the forested shore of Tawnyard Lough. On emerging from the forest, a road leads up to a fine viewpoint taking in more of Connemara's spectacular mountain scenery. This narrow road later clings to a steep, rocky slope as it descends towards Sheefry Bridge. There's a rough walk ahead, as the Western Way climbs towards a rocky gap in the mountains at about 420m. The descent is steep and rocky and care is needed to reach Lugacolliwee Lough. Tussocky moorlands have been recently turned over for forestry, so follow a river downstream from Lugacolliwee Lough to reach a road at Tawnyslinnaun. In foul weather, a waymarked road can be used from Sheefry Bridge to Tawnyslinnaun.

The road is followed to a junction, where another road leads uphill. A series of low, boggy hills are crossed, and the shapely cone of Croagh Patrick is always directly ahead. A forest fence is followed to the lower slopes of the mountain, then a track leads through the forest to join a minor road. If you want to climb to the summit of Croagh Patrick, then it's best to reserve a day for the task. You'll be too worn out to do it after this day's walk. Roads lead towards Westport, a busy little town with a splendid range of facilities. There is a youth hostel in town, though you might opt for the first B & B you see.

A view along Tawnyard Lough to the Mweelrea Mountains

(*overleaf*) The round tower which rises above the centre of town in Killala

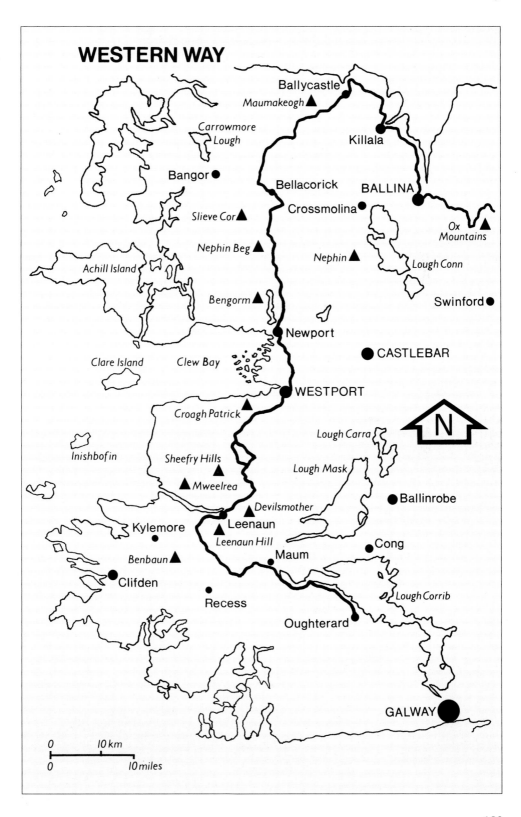

Westport to Treanlaur Lodge

16 miles (26km)

In complete contrast to yesterday's walk, today's walk is almost entirely along roads and keeps its distance from the mountains. You might find time to visit Westport House before leaving town. There is a short walk along an overgrown track, then quiet roads lead through rolling drumlin country. Where the drumlins reach the sea at Clew Bay, they form a spread of tiny islands – reputedly one for every day of the year. The church at the tiny village of Fahy is a landmark by which you can gauge your progress.

Newport is only a small town, but it has a good range of shops, pubs and lodgings. Rather than crossing the road bridge to enter town, you could cross an old railway viaduct which is open to the public. On the way out of Newport, there are both yellow and green waymarks along the roads. The yellow ones are for the Western Way, while the green ones mark the Bangor Trail. Both pursue the same course at first, later using a track called the Rocky Road to reach a high-level road overlooking Lough Feeagh. The only accommodation hereabouts is Treanlaur Lodge Youth Hostel, which is reached by a short detour from the route.

Treanlaur Lodge to Bellacorick

17 miles (27km)

You can look on the Bangor Trail as a spur from the Western Way, or as a separate walk with its own guidebook. The Bangor Trail follows an old drove road across the western slopes of the Nephin Beg Range, while the Western Way follows an easier series of forest tracks across the eastern slopes of the mountains. The parting of the two ways occurs beyond Srahmore Lodge.

The Western Way follows tracks close to the Altaconey River for a while, then climbs gently between a couple of low hills. There are views of Nephin, in the middle of the Nephin Beg Range, and the hill known as Slieve Cor, which is the highest of the range. Far away across the forest and broad bogs is the cooling tower of the Bellacorick Power Station. A recent addition to the Bellacorick scene is a wind farm.

Getting to Bellacorick is simply a matter of following forest tracks, then minor roads, then the main road onwards to the tiny village. The problem is, there's no accommodation. You can obtain food and drink while waiting for a bus to Bangor, or you could hitchhike there. If you've any time to spare, you could try and get a tune out of the Musical Bridge outside the village!

Bellacorick to Ballycastle

22 miles (36km)

The main road is followed away from Bellacorick, then a long track leads across a black bogland which is being worked for fuel. Mixed woodlands are reached at Sheskin, an estate now managed as a nature reserve. Forest tracks continue onwards, passing ruined farmsteads before it becomes necessary to cross some wet, grassy moorlands. Most of this boggy area has been turned over for forestry, but the trees have only been planted recently. A forest track leads down to an abandoned farmhouse near the Altderg River. A difficult stretch follows. First, the edge of a forest is traced, then an overgrown forest ride leads gradually uphill on the broad slopes of Maumakeogh. This can be wet, with hidden ditches and branches waiting to trip the unwary walker.

After fording a stream, a forest track runs above Glencullen and leads walkers quickly downhill to join a minor road. Ballycastle is soon reached and this little village has shops, pubs and B & Bs. Views ahead include coastal cliffs, marking a change of theme in the course of the Western Way.

Ballycastle to Ballina

25 miles (40km)

The whole of this day's walk is along roads, with occasional views of the sea or distant mountain ranges. Leaving Ballycastle, a road leads to Ballycastle Beach. You have the option of detouring to Downpatrick Head, where St Patrick forced all the snakes in Ireland to fall into the sea after his forty day fast on the summit of Croagh Patrick! Later, the road climbs over a low hill which offers a fine view of Nephin, Bireencorragh and the Nephin Beg Range. Apart from the odd ruined church, look out for stone circles and ancient burial tombs. Some are close to the road, so are easy to visit.

Minor roads are used to reach Killala, by which time you'll have been reminded of the French landing of 1798. The little town has a round tower and a small cathedral. If you want to break this long day into two shorter days, then there are lodgings available. History continues to be an important theme on the road walk to Ballina, with Moyne Abbey and Rosserk Abbey being reached by short detours. After passing through an impressive gatehouse, Ballina is finally reached. This large town is quite busy and has a full range of facilities for weary walkers.

Ballina to Lough Talt

15 miles (24km)

Roads are followed away from Ballina, quiet minor roads which eventually reach the Ox Mountains at Ellagh. Here, as a fine track climbs across rugged slopes and passes small forests, there's a view across Lough Conn to the distant Nephins. An old road crosses and recrosses the main road running through a gap in the Ox Mountains. The final part of this line is rough and boggy. The Western Way ends suddenly at a sign welcoming motorists to the west of Ireland. For a more scenic ending, you might be inclined to cross the gap and reach Lough Talt. Eventually, the route might be extended and could ultimately be linked with the distant Ulster Way.

WESTERN WAY INFORMATION

Schedule:

	miles	km
Oughterard – Maum BB	15	24
Maum – Leenaun BB	20	32
Leenaun – Westport YH	25	40
Westport – Treanlaur Lodge YH	16	26
Treanlaur Lodge – Bellacorick	17	27
Bellacorick – Ballycastle BB	22	36
Ballycastle – Ballina BB	25	40
Ballina – Lough Talt BB	15	24
Total distance	155	249

Maps:

OSI 1:50,000 Rambler Sheets 23, 24, 31, 32, 37, 38 & 45.
Half Inch Sheets 6, 7 & 11.

Guidebooks:

A West of Ireland Walk Guide – The Western Way, by Joe McDermott and Robert Chapman, published by Mayo County Council.

Accommodation List:

Bord Failte.

Tourist Information Centres:

Galway, Leenaun, Westport, Newport, Killala, Ballina.

The Ulster Way (Donegal Section) (map pp.192-3)

The Ulster Way which crosses the length of Co Donegal ties in with the enormous Ulster Way circuit around Northern Ireland. The link is at the small border town of Pettigo. Don't be fooled into thinking that this is going to be an easy walk because it only measures 69 miles (111km). There are indeed some easy stretches along forest tracks and minor roads, but there are also some very rugged, boggy moorlands and mountainsides to cross too. It might be fair to say that this is one of the more difficult trails and in bad weather your navigation needs to be spot on. Waymarks are often widely spaced and there are rivers which may be difficult to ford after heavy rain.

The route runs from Pettigo to the Atlantic coast at Falcarragh and the distance could be covered in less than a week. Accommodation is sparse, but there are a few B & Bs and a youth hostel available. Backpackers could easily seek permission for pitches, or might establish discreet camps in the wilds. You can't camp in state forests or the Glenveagh National Park. Shopping opportunities are limited and there are only a couple of pubs on the route. Provided that your plans are well thought out, and that you're fit enough and well equipped for the trip, then there should be no problems. At the time of writing, the northern stretch wasn't waymarked, though for some time the county council have been supplying details of the proposed route.

Pettigo to Lough Eske

18 miles (29km)

You'll need to do some shopping in Pettigo as the next shops near the route are in Fintown. Pettigo is only a small place, but it tends to have two of everything because the border runs through it. The start of the trail is easy, simply follow the road which runs towards Lough Derg. In summer there could be a fair amount of traffic as pilgrims head for Lough Derg, and a roadside refreshment hut might be open. You don't go all the way to Lough Derg, but follow a minor road into the Crocknacunny Forest. There is an alternative, rather longer route planned around the shore of Lough Derg for the future. Look out for a glimpse of Station Island, where thousands of pilgrims endure 'St Patrick's Purgatory' every year. Walking barefoot around the island, they pray and fast for three days and two nights. One night is spent without sleep and the fasting continues after leaving the island too. Pilgrims often return year after year to complete this arduous ritual.

Keep an eye open for waymarks on the walk through the forest. There are several junctions to pass at first, then the trail leaves a firm track for a while to sample some rather soft ground. At a junction near Kelly's Bridge, close to the border, a track runs northwards and follows a broad, boggy forest ride all the way to the edge of the forest. There's a rugged moorland walk at about 300m, then a good bog road is joined. This track keeps well above the Clogher River and offers fine views over the wooded shores of Lough Eske and the rocky ridge of the Blue Stack Mountains. There are only a couple of B & Bs by the roadside at Lough Eske, but there's a road leading off-route to Donegal town if a fuller range of services are required.

(*overleaf*) **Rugged bogland stretches away towards the Barnesmore Gap**

Lough Eske to Fintown

22 miles (36km)

The road walk by Lough Eske gradually leads uphill around the northern end of the lake. A farm access track runs up to a water intake above a fine waterfall. The Ulster Way forges onwards into a boggy, rocky valley, following the river to its head on a broad gap at about 300m. In fine weather, you'll be able to see the next part of the trail, but in misty weather there's an awkward move to be made. The route crosses from one gap to another, slightly higher gap. Waymarks are widely spread and there's no trodden path. The descent to the Owendoo River also crosses trackless wastes. The river needs to be forded, which can be very difficult when it's in spate. Once across, walk over a broad, boggy rise to reach the scattered farms of Letterkillew.

The Ulster Way doesn't cross the Owengarve River, but follows it upstream to reach a broad gap at the head of the Poldoo Glen. No one would blame you for using the farm and forest track across the river, which also leads close to the gap. The trail descends to another area of scattered farmsteads known as The Croaghs. These are lined alongside the Reelan River. A firm farm access track leads towards the head of the valley, with good views of the rugged Blue Stack Mountains.

Take care on the walk across Croveenananta, as the trail crosses hummocky moors and small streams where the line could easily be lost. There's a road and a river to cross, then a track rises from a bridge to join a minor road. This road can be followed to Fintown, offering splendid views across Lough Muck and Lough Finn. Fintown is a long, straggly village, but a walk through it ultimately reveals a couple of shops, pubs and B & Bs.

Fintown to Dunlewy

17 miles (27km)

A road walk from Fintown passes through a forest and leads to small, isolated farms. A track continues through a broad, boggy valley which has been recently turned over for forestry. Eventually, a couple of isolated ruins are reached and the trail leaves the firm track to cross the empty moors. Markers are usually far apart and you'll need to look for them carefully. After climbing uphill, aim for Lough Muck. Next, try and locate the course of the Ulster Way as it wanders around the rugged slopes of Crockastoller. A rocky river is followed to its source at about 425m on a boggy gap. Careful attention should be paid to the route as it heads for a high gap between Moylenanav and the Glenveagh National Park.

Cross the road on the high gap and make a rugged ascent towards the Derryveagh Mountains. There's a tall deer fence, but a gate gives access to the higher parts of the mountains. Keep climbing to reach a broad, rocky, boggy gap. Great care is needed to locate a safe descent towards the Poisoned Glen. The route is steep, wet and slippery. At the foot of this slope, the boggy floor of the glen is surrounded by huge, boilerplate slabs of granite. There's no gate in the lower deer fence, so you'll have to breathe in and slip between the wire strands. Climbing it is not recommended. After leaving the Poisoned Glen, a minor road leads through the scattered village of Dunlewy. There are a youth hostel, a couple of B & Bs, a shop and pub – just enough to keep body and soul together.

A ruined tower house by Altan Lough at the foot of Aghla More

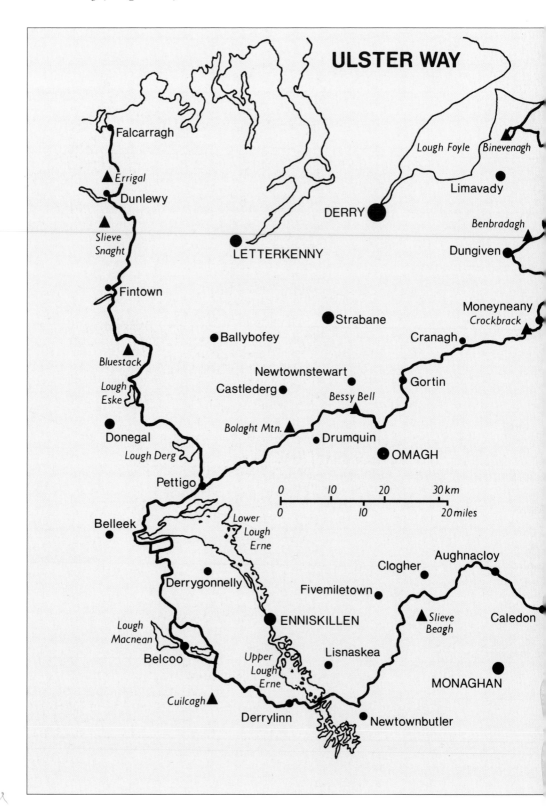

Dunlewy to Falcarragh

12 miles (19km)

In the morning, follow the road uphill and enjoy the view over Dunlewy Lough and the old, roofless church. If you're bursting with energy, then you could climb to the summit of Errigal as an optional extra. The trail leads along a boggy track from the roadside, heading over a rise to a remote tower-house at the head of Altan Lough. There is a river to cross near a waterfall. The Ulster Way follows the shore of Altan Lough, around the foot of the steep-sided Aghla More. The path is narrow and rocky in places, with some boggy parts towards the end. A minor road is joined beyond the foot of the lake, which runs roughly parallel with the Tullaghobegly River. There are glimpses of the Atlantic Ocean ahead, but the little village of Falcarragh is reached just beforehand. There are plenty of shops and pubs, a couple of B & Bs and an independent hostel.

ULSTER WAY (DONEGAL SECTION) INFORMATION

Schedule:

	miles	km
Pettigo – Lough Eske BB	18	29
Lough Eske – Fintown BB	22	36
Fintown – Dunlewy YH	17	27
Dunlewy – Falcarragh IH	12	19
Total distance	69	111

Maps:

OSI 1:50,000 Rambler Sheets 1, 6 & 11. OSNI 1:50,000 Discoverer Sheets 12 & 17.

Guidebooks:

None, but notes describing the route are available from Donegal County Council. Also useful is *Walking the Ulster Way*, by Alan Warner, published by Appletree Press Ltd.

Accommodation List:

Bord Failte.

Tourist Information Centres:

Donegal, Letterkenny.

Northern Ireland

◆

The Ulster Way

(map pp.192-3)

The Ulster Way is an enormous circular trail around Northern Ireland. It passes through all six counties of Northern Ireland, with some short stretches across the border in Co Donegal and Co Cavan. Basically, the trail includes: a tour through the Antrim Mountains and glens; the spectacular North Antrim Coast Path; the forests and moors of the Sperrin Mountains; the Fermanagh Lakelands; the Rivers Blackwater and Bann; the Newry Canal; the lofty Mountains of Mourne; and various parts of the Co Down coastline. The scenery is remarkably varied and several stretches of the route lie in Areas of Outstanding Natural Beauty – Antrim Coast and Glens; Causeway Coast; North Derry; Sperrin; Erne Lakeland (proposed); Fermanagh Caveland (proposed); Lecale Coast; Strangford Lough; and Lagan Valley.

Few walkers could hope to complete the circuit in a single journey and only a handful have done so (author included). To make things easier, the route has been broken into five sections which could each be covered in a week or so by wayfarers: North Eastern; North Western; South Western; Southern; and South Eastern. Further breakdowns offer individual trails which could be completed over a weekend, or even in a day, including: The North Sperrin Trail; The Big Dog Trail; St Patrick's Trail; etc. If you were drawn to walk the whole route at once, it would probably take up to five weeks.

There is abundant accommodation in many popular areas – most notably around the coast. There are a few youth hostels and camp-sites, with plentiful B & Bs available. On the inland stretches, there are no youth hostels, very few camp-sites, and B & Bs can be rather sparse. In some places, there is simply no accommodation at all, though backpackers should always be able to negotiate successfully for a pitch. You might be faced with lengthy detours for B & B. If there's a handy bus service, then there's no problem, but hitchhiking to distant accommodation on virtually traffic-free minor roads can take some time. One little trick of the trade is to negotiate your accommodation in advance, and ask if you can be collected by car from a particular road junction. It takes a great deal of planning, but could save plenty of time and effort. Similarly, food and drink can be hard to obtain on some inland stretches. You shouldn't have to walk more than two or three days without being able to buy something, but it's handy to know where the gaps are so that you can stock up in advance.

At the time of writing, there is no complete guidebook to the Ulster Way. The course of the entire trail is shown accurately on the 1:250,000 Holiday Map of Ireland – North. There are a series of little leaflets and booklets which cover most of the route in varying detail, but other parts haven't a word of coverage. What you'll end up with is a sort of mobile library of leaflets, booklets, maps and incidental guidebooks. There's a specific accommodation list for the route called *An Information Guide to Accommodation for Walkers on the Ulster Way*. This is published by the Northern Ireland Tourist Board and includes a range of hotels, B & Bs, youth hostels and camp-sites. A 'walking man' symbol is used to denote accommodation which is fairly handy for the route. Add this to your mobile library and you should have everything you need to complete the walk.

Some walkers could be unwilling to tackle the Ulster Way because of the amount of violence reported from Northern Ireland. However, you're more likely to be at risk from the old favourites – bad weather, benightedness and a broken leg. Read Alan Warner's book about the Ulster Way, which illustrates how readily people will come to the aid of the struggling wayfarer. The distance is quoted from 500 miles (805km) to 600 miles (965km). It probably measures about 570 miles (917km) and in practice turns out to be a little longer.

Dunmurry to Whiteabbey

17 miles (27km)

You could, of course, start the Ulster Way at any point, but Belfast is easily reached and Dunmurry is only a short bus or rail journey from the centre of the city. West Belfast is negotiated first and its suburbs vary from pleasant to grim. Once you've followed the Suffolk Road uphill, you'll be well above the city and walking along a country road. An access track leads to a TV mast and beyond that is the 360m summit of Black Hill. A pathless and sometimes boggy walk leads to 390m Black Mountain, then after passing another TV mast there's a climb towards Divis. There's a military installation on the 478m summit and from time to time this part of the route could be closed. If that happens, you can detour around the lower slopes of the hill.

After crossing a road the Ulster Way goes over Squires Hill. Cross another road, then aim for Cave Hill. McArt's Fort, a fine promontory fort, overlooks the city and the view could detain you for some time. Although there's a popular path leading downhill nearby, the trail stays fairly high for a while and descends above Belfast Zoo. You'll see some strange animals on this walk! After wandering through a suburb of the city, there's a short, wooded, riverside walk which leads to a coastal walk along the shore of Belfast Lough. This joins a busy road at Whiteabbey, where you'll be able to find food, drink and accommodation. Alternatively, you could stay anywhere in Belfast and catch a bus to join the trail at Whiteabbey in the morning.

Whiteabbey to Ballynure

13 miles (21km)

There's still a bit of the urban sprawl to walk through, but after a grim start at Whiteabbey the lovely Three Mile Water leads walkers clear of Newtownabbey. Minor roads and farm tracks run uphill and a detour could be made to the lofty war memorial on Knockagh. Views over Belfast Lough from there are excellent. The memorial is a little off-route, and the Ulster

Way goes along paths and tracks through the Woodburn Forest. There's a walk alongside a small reservoir, and later a track climbs to 270m in North Carn Forest. Follow a path downhill past farms. Roads have to be walked to reach Ballynure, where you can break for food, drink and B & B. It's unwise to continue as there are bleak moorlands ahead.

Ballynure to Glenarm

20 miles (32km)

Minor roads describe sweeping zigzags past houses and farms to take the trail up to Ballyboley Forest. Tracks and a forest ride lead over the 366m summit of Carninard, then, after descending to cross a road, the Ulster Way follows forest paths to emerge on a broad, bleak moorland. Waymarks are widely spaced, but the route is simply a matter of aiming for

the high ground and crossing 474m Agnews Hill. A steep face overlooks Larne Harbour, while broad moorlands spread away inland to end with the striking little hump of Slemish where St Patrick worked as a pigherd.

After descending steeply to cross a road, a hummocky moorland walk leads to a standing stone near another road. Across the road is some rugged moorland, then the semicircular cliff line of Sallagh Braes is reached suddenly. There are fine views to Ballygally Head, but the youth hostel there is perhaps too far off-route to be useful. Stay high and pass the site of a promontory fort on Knock Dhu, then descend and cross a road on a gap.

A climb uphill reaches a broad crest crowned with various hummocks. Eventually, the route leads to the 381m summit of Black Hill. Take care on the descent, aiming for the rise called Crockandoo before joining a road. The road gradually descends to Glenarm, which has a few shops, pubs and B & Bs. If you can't find a place to stay, then continue to nearby Carnlough. Glenarm is the first of the Nine Glens of Antrim. Although the trail doesn't actually enter every glen, you should be able to see all nine of them. You'll catch a glimpse of Glenarm Castle while exploring town.

Glenarm to Cushendall

14 miles (22km)

A minor road keeps above the main coastal road to lead from Glenarm to Carnlough. You could break here for food and drink and have a look at the town wall before embarking on a moorland trek. The climb uphill starts gently by following a road above Cranny Falls. You won't really see the falls before a track starts zigzagging up past the last farms. Eventually, the trail passes between the humps of Big Trosk and Little Trosk to reach an undulating, lough-strewn moorland. In mist you'll need to navigate carefully and watch the widely spaced waymarks. Denny's Lough, Loughnacally and Lough Natullig are passed in turn, then a steep descent alongside Altmore Burn leads to a road in Glenariff.

A simple road walk leads down the glen, then a coastal road is followed through the village of Waterfoot. A minor road is used to avoid the coast road, climbing above the Red Arch and leading quietly into Cushendall. This little town is known as the 'Capital of the Glens'. It offers shops, pubs, B & Bs, youth hostel and camp-site.

Cushendall to Ballycastle

20 miles (32km)

There's a short coastal walk near Cushendall, with good views back to the steep-sided mountain of Lurigethan. A step inland at the ruined Layd Church takes the trail along a minor road crossing the slopes of Cross Slieve. A descent leads into Cushendun, which has plenty of National Trust buildings. There's food and drink on offer while you're exploring, and note that there's nothing else until you reach Ballycastle.

A road zigzags uphill, but a track is used to miss out a wide bend. The track is an old road and its course can be followed to 300m on the higher moors. There's a gradual descent which may or may not include a view of Loughareema – known as the Vanishing Lake because it frequently drains away down a sort of natural plughole. Part way up the next rise the old road is left and the route forges uphill until it reaches an ancient burial chamber on the 379m summit of Carnanmore. Views are remarkable and include places far removed from the Antrim Mountains. Great tracts of Scotland can be seen.

Walk down to cross a road, then wander over Greenanmore to pick up a spectacular cliff walk around Fair Head. Sheer cliffs fall down to massive aprons of boulders which slope into the sea. Rathlin Island can be seen across the Moyle. There's a descent from the top of the cliff to a lower path and this leads easily around Colliery Bay to reach Ballycastle. The town has a full range of services, including an independent hostel. If the day has been clear, then you'll have seen the last of the Nine Glens of Antrim. If you've never eaten yellow man or dulse, then try some while in town.

Ballycastle to Portballintrae

19 miles (31km)

The walk along the North Antrim Coast starts with a disappointing road walk from Ballycastle. After some time it moves closer to the sea and a detour can include the celebrated Carrick-a-Rede Island and its airy suspension footbridge (removed each winter). You can take a break at Ballintoy, then pass a lovely whitewashed church before a sudden corkscrew descent by road to Ballintoy Port. The sea is filled with grotesque shattered stacks and a path threads its way between a handful which are marooned on a raised beach. You won't be able to get round the headland if the tide is fully in, but once around there's a walk along a broad strand around White Park Bay. If you're fascinated by this area, then there's a youth hostel you could stay at above the bay.

Look out for the smallest church in Ireland in a garden at Portbradden, then go through a hole in a headland at Gid Point. There's a climb up to the main coast road, giving a view of the ruined Dunseverick Castle on a shattered headland. The North Antrim Coast Path wanders around Benbane Head to reach the immensely popular Giant's Gauseway. You can either stay on the top of the cliffs or follow an exciting path which has been cut out of a weak band halfway down the cliff. Either way, go down to the sea and study all those crazy, hexagonal columns that have made the place so interesting and appealing.

There's a visitor centre on the cliff top where you can discover all about the Giant's Causeway – its legends, history, formation and importance as a tourist attraction. There's also food and drink available. The path leading onwards to Portballintrae seems very tame after all the recent excitement. Low cliffs and a golf course are crossed on the way to the little seaside resort.

The crazy columns of the Giant's Causeway – an immensely popular place

NORTH WESTERN SECTION

Portballintrae to Castlerock

22 miles (36km)

This is a long day's walk, but it's also low lying and mostly routed along roads. You could call an early halt at either Portrush, Portstewart or Coleraine. To start the day's walk, leave Portballintrae by road and head for the spectacular ruins of Dunluce Castle. The coastline beyond the castle is impressive, but you'll have to study it from the roadside. Later, you can leave the road and walk around Curran Strand to reach Portrush. There's an interesting countryside centre next to a rocky shoreline nature reserve in town.

This resort has a full range of services and is attractively sited on a headland. A promenade path leaves town, then a crinkly coastline leads towards Portstewart. This is another popular resort with plenty of facilities, including an independent hostel. A school and chapel are situated on a rocky headland and a path leads beneath the crenellated walls.

The mouth of the River Bann has no ferry service, so the Ulster Way heads inland to find a bridge at Coleraine. There's a ruined church on the outskirts of Portstewart, then the trail passes the New University of Ulster. You could explore Coleraine before crossing a splendid bridge over the River Bann. A minor road keeps walkers off the main road and leads over the low rise of Cranagh Hill. Flat country is crossed by the Articlave River, then a road leads straight into Castlerock. This is the last resort on the north coast, and the last opportunity to visit the shops before distant Dungiven. There are a range of lodgings available.

Castlerock to Formoyle

17 miles (28km)

The day starts with a short cliff walk and a view of the folly called Mussenden Temple. Just inland is the enormous ruin of Downhill, built by the Earl Bishop of Bristol and Derry. The whole area is now managed by the National Trust. The sea is left behind and the Ulster Way starts a long march inland towards the Sperrin Mountains. There is a short walk through a beautifully wooded valley, then the climbing starts. Once above the woods, the trail follows the straight line of the Bishop's Road up to Eagle Hill and Windy Hill. There is a magnificent viewpoint overlooking Lough Foyle and the hills of Donegal. A nearby plaque commemorates how the Ordnance Survey started mapping the whole of Ireland from a base line marked out beside Lough Foyle.

The route continues along the Bishop's Road, then there's a circuit of Binevenagh to complete. This involves a forest walk to Binevenagh Lake, near the summit of the hill, followed by a walk along a cliff edge before descending back into the forest. The trail rejoins the Bishop's Road after sampling wide-ranging views.

A road leads past a couple of TV masts, reaching 350m on Harkin's Hill. Several stretches of forested moorlands lie ahead, starting with a gradual descent through Grange Park Wood. A road is joined at the ominously named Murder Hole. Travellers were once robbed, killed and dumped by this roadside. The road leads over to Formoyle and you should have worked out where you are going to stay for the night. There is a B & B a little off-route at Ballinrees, or you could try and get a lift to Coleraine or Limavady for all the services those towns can supply.

Atlantic breakers pound the cliffs beneath the folly of Mussenden Temple

Formoyle to Dungiven

22 miles (36km)

Formoyle is only a few houses and a chapel, with a road leading into a forest. There are all sorts of junctions to watch as you go through Springwell Forest, but after crossing a main road a more direct track goes over to Cam forest, reaching 320m on the way. After following a road downhill in the direction of Ringsend, a series of forest tracks lead uphill and out of the forest. There's a short, difficult moorland walk on Temain Hill, with a road being used to reach 360m near some masts. The road runs downhill and another road crosses Coolnasillagh River before heading uphill. After running through a forest, the road bends around a hollow called Legavannon Pot and continues down to a roadside pub.

A minor road runs uphill from the pub and the Ulster Way crosses a hill slope to link two parts of Gortnamoyagh Forest. A road goes past another hollow, this one being called Legananam Pot. A quiet road runs uphill to cross a broad shoulder of Benbradagh to reach Dungiven. It's a quiet road because it's closed to traffic. Benbradagh used to bristle with communications masts planted by US forces, but these have all been removed and only the anchorage points remain. After reaching an altitude of 420m, the road zigzags steeply downhill. A more gentle course finally leads to Dungiven. There are plenty of shops and pubs, plus a limited number of lodgings offered.

Dungiven to Moneyneany

12 miles (19km)

There's a stretch along roads beyond Dungiven, but at least the busy Glenshane road doesn't have to be followed too far and quiet roads are used to cross the River Roe. A clear track runs around the lower slopes of Corick Mountain to reach Glenshane Forest. It was obviously once a good highway, but the moorland is gradually reclaiming it. Forest tracks climb steadily and remain close to the headwaters of the River Roe. After a final steep

The rugged slopes of Benbradagh are crossed on the way to Dungiven

Moneyneany to Cranagh

14 miles (22km)

A twisting minor road leaves Moneyneany and a farm track continues uphill. Finally, a zigzag track climbs up the open hillside and reaches the 478m summit of Crockmore. There are wide-ranging views around the Sperrin Mountains and a great expanse of lower ground can be studied. The trail leads across Crockbrack, then descends the boggy slopes of the hill and crosses Glengomna Water. Roads are followed for the rest of the day. These lead over bleak moorlands at the head of Glenelly, then pass Goles Forest and scattered farms to reach the tiny village of Sperrin. There's a pub at that point, and a change onto a minor road. The road goes above one side of Glenelly, passing several farms. The small village of Cranagh is on the opposite side of the valley. As it has a small shop, pub and solitary B & B, it's worth wandering off-route to reach it. If you've any spare time, then pay a visit to the nearby Sperrin Heritage Centre.

Cranagh to Mountjoy

22 miles (35km)

There seems to be no end to the road walking through Glenelly. The Ulster Way continues along minor roads, staying fairly high and passing small farms. Suddenly, it runs uphill through the Barnes Gap and crosses to a very wide valley. There's a length of stony track to follow, then it's back onto tarmac to reach Gortin. There are shops, pubs and limited lodgings in Gortin if the walk needs to be broken early.

A lovely path follows a small river upstream to reach Gortin Glen Forest Park. There's a small firing range by the forest, but the trail stays clear of any danger and climbs uphill on good tracks. There's a sudden descent to cross a road, then the route leads close to a refresh-

climb there's a boggy gap to cross at nearly 450m. On the descent, pick up a track which runs straight down through Moydamlaght Forest. The forest is left at a picnic site and a simple road walk leads into Moneyneany. There's food and drink, but no accommodation. Either head off-route to Draperstown for lodgings or walk all the way to Cranagh.

ment hut. There is a forest camp-site, which backpackers might want to note. Anyone with bags of spare time could detour to the Ulster History Park at Cullion.

To continue along the Ulster Way, paths lead upstream along Pollan Burn to reach 400m at My Lady's Viewpoint. A broad track runs straight downhill to leave the forest at Rosnamuck. Roads have to be followed across

Stone Bridge to Mountjoy and the Ulster American Folk Park. There are a few B & Bs in the area, including Camphill Farm, where the Mellon family homestead is preserved. The Mellons went to America and founded a banking empire, and many other Ulster-American links are celebrated at the folk park. There is a shop just off-route in Mountjoy village.

Mountjoy to Lough Bradan Forest

24 miles (38km)

A busy road by the Ulster American Folk Park is avoided as the trail leads along a quieter minor road near the Strule River. Roads climb uphill near the Mellon Country Inn and lead to Upper Beltany. Then climb up a rugged moorland slope to reach the 420m summit of Bessy Bell. There's a mast on top, served by a road which is used for the descent into Baronscourt Forest. The trail is back on tarmac roads by the time it's passing a small church. These roads lead to Drumlegagh, where there are decisions to be made.

In this tiny village there's a last chance to do some shopping before distant Pettigo is reached. The only accommodation anywhere near the Ulster Way is the Inn at Baronscourt. Even starting from there in the morning, it's a very long walk to Pettigo.

The road runs downhill from Drumlegagh to cross Fairy Water, then more roads lead up through Kilmore. Your options are becoming very limited; you could move well off-route by bus to stay at Castlederg which has the reputation of being a 'bitter little town'. Once you start climbing uphill on minor roads you're quickly on a moorland road and committed to passing the last few buildings. The trail leads over a rugged moorland on Bolaght Mountain. Lonely Lough Lee is passed and the route climbs over the crest of the moors to enter Lough Bradan Forest. A series of forest tracks run up and downhill, but eventually exit onto a road. There's no accommodation closer than a solitary B & B off-route at Gortnagullion.

SOUTH WESTERN SECTION

Lough Bradan Forest to Pettigo

12 miles (19km)

The South Western Section of the Ulster Way is routed through Co Fermanagh, where waymarks and stiles are often painted with fluorescent orange paint so that you can see them in the low light of forests and hedgerows. There's also a greater effort made to keep the route off the roads, but as you'll discover while walking through Kesh Forest, you could end up in deep mud at times.

It's a fiddly route along farm roads and forest tracks, while in more open country the

trail crosses low hills overlooking Termon River, which marks the border in this area. Some of the paths are hard to follow, so keep your eyes peeled. Eventually, a minor road is followed and this leads across a border bridge which is barred to vehicles. This is Pettigo, a border village which, as a result, has two of most things. All the pubs and B & Bs, however, are found on the Co Donegal side. There's also another Ulster Way, leading northwards through Co Donegal to the Atlantic coast at Falcarragh.

Pettigo to Rosscor

14 miles (23km)

A road walk leads away from Pettigo, but the trail also includes a short track. Beyond a roadside pub, a border bridge has been demolished to prevent its use by vehicles. The Ulster Way is routed across the river by way of an old railway viaduct. You can't help feeling furtive but this is the official route. Minor roads lead to Tullyvocady, then a forest track continues into low, hilly country. A series of markers show the way across a moorland, then a minor road is followed to Croaghdotia. A difficult walk traces a river downstream and ends with a good, firm farm track. A road walk passes Lough Scolban, then heads for a ruined church on a hill top. Descend through woodlands to reach the entry to Castle Caldwell Forest.

Castle Caldwell is worth a short detour, but as it's on a narrow peninsula jutting into Lower Lough Erne you'll have to retrace your steps afterwards. An old railway trackbed leaves the forest to run to Rosscor. There are odd B & Bs in this area, but all are off-route. You might end up having to go to Belleek for a bed, but at least it has a full range of facilities. Occasional buses could save you a walk in and out of town.

Rosscor to Doagh Glebe

16 miles (25km)

A sign at Rosscor says that the bridge is closed. In fact, it's open, but a missing span has been replaced with a wooden hump. There's a huge army checkpoint at a road junction, which you'll have to go through even though you're not crossing the border. Once through, there's a little shop by the road – you won't see another shop until Belcoo or Derrylinn, depending on your later choice of routes.

There's a minor choice of routes almost immediately. You can either climb straight uphill to the Barr of Whealt, or walk along roads past Legg House and climb a flight of steps to the top of the Cliffs of Magho. The Magho viewpoint is finer, but requires a longer walk to reach. It overlooks Lower Lough Erne and the distant hills of Donegal. Both routes later converge and paths and tracks lead past Meenameen Lough. This is Lough Navar Forest, and Lough Navar is visited later. Occasionally, the trail crosses a forest drive which allows cars to travel to the Magho viewpoint. The Ulster Way is taken past an old 'sweat house' which has an explanatory notice showing how it was used as a sort of sauna.

The trail descends near a farm and crosses a road. A stretch of rugged country follows, with areas of forest, moorlands, and short, steep ups and downs. It's very scenic, but hard work too. Keep an eye on the waymarks to reach a minor road at Doagh Glebe. If you're looking for B & B accommodation, then it's best to go off-route to Derrygonnelly. Although the village is within walking distance, it would be better if you could arrange to be collected. Hardly any traffic uses the road.

Doagh Glebe to Belcoo

16 miles (25km)

After a short road walk from Doagh Glebe, the Ulster Way heads into the Big Dog Forest and wanders off the main track to visit a couple of lovely little pools. There are two steep and rough climbs onto Little Dog and Big Dog – isolated hills with superb views of the surrounding countryside. It's a struggle to reach a nearby road as the path is very muddy. The next forest is traversed mostly on good, clear tracks. There's a brief walk on open moorlands between Lough Formal and Lough Namanfin. As the Ulster Way heads downhill on good tracks again there's a choice of routes to consider, depending on your nightime needs.

One route wanders out of the forest near the solitary Holywell Church and goes down a road to reach Holywell and Belcoo. This border village has shops, pubs and a few B & Bs on offer, which most walkers would find attractive. The disadvantage is in the amount of road walking required to reach it. The other route stays in the forest longer, crossing a minor road and continuing through Belmore Forest on a good track. There's a descent along farm tracks around Cleggan to reach a main road some distance from Belcoo. The nearest B & B to the route is at Abocurragh.

The Little Dog viewpoint, which takes in the whole north west of Ireland

Belcoo to Derrylinn

23 miles (37km)

The Belcoo route starts by crossing the border to reach the village of Blacklion, then crosses the border again to head along a minor road to Claddagh Bridge. The other route enjoys a shore walk around Lough Macnean Lower, though the path could be flooded after heavy rain. The River Claddagh is followed to Claddagh Bridge.

With both routes now converged, the Ulster Way climbs up into the scenic, wooded Claddagh Glen. There is a nature trail to note, which leads over a rock formation known as the Marble Arch. The Marble Arch Caves are immediately to hand, though you have to go to a nearby visitor centre before going underground. There is a small restaurant on site, if you're looking for a meal. If you do explore the caves, then you'll probably not be able to reach distant Derrylinn by the end of the day. There is a B & B in the direction of Florence Court.

The trail follows a minor road downhill, then paths lead back uphill and cross a hummocky slope before briefly entering Florence Court Forest. By following the edge of the forest, a sign will be reached which marks the start of the 'hikers trail' to the summit of Cuilcagh. This remote and rugged mountain was once going to be included in the Ulster Way, but it's now reserved for hardy walkers who have the time and energy to tackle it. Yellow markers lead to the summit, then you're on your own.

The Ulster Way charts a lower course on the slopes of nearby Benaughlin. A forest track leads down to a road, then odd roads and tracks are linked on the way towards Kinawley. The trail doesn't actually enter the village, but bypasses it by cutting over a patch of bogland. The village has food and drink, if you want to detour for it. Roads signposted as a scenic drive lead across the slopes of Molly Mountain to cross a gap in the hills at Doon. If you've time to spare you might like to climb by road to a higher viewpoint, but you can already see across the island-studded Upper Lough Erne. Roads lead straight down to Derrylinn. Accommodation is limited to a single hotel, but in desperation you could get a bus to Enniskillen for a full range of services. Derrylinn also has shops, which won't feature again on the Ulster Way until Aughnacloy is reached.

Derrylinn to Newtownbutler

13 miles (21km)

Accommodation is going to be a problem over the next few days, so think ahead. On this day's stretch, there's nothing actually on the route, but there are lodgings in the surrounding countryside. If you walk from Derrylinn to Newtownbutler, you'll be able to get a bus to as far away as Lisnaskea in search of a place to stay. It's a short day's walk, almost entirely by road, so you should be able to find time to sort out something for the evening.

Follow a minor road from Derrylinn, then join a busier road to cross Upper Lough Erne by way of Lady Brooke Bridge and Lady Craigavon Bridge. There's a path between the bridges which goes around the shore of Trasna Island. Another shore-path almost reaches the Share Centre – an outdoor activity centre for disabled people. Watch for waymarks as the road wanders from Drumguiff Cross Roads to Derryadd, then through Drumlone to pass two crossroads before reaching a main road. Newtownbutler is off-route, but it has shops and pubs. If you can't obtain lodgings there, then get a bus to Lisnaskea, but check the bus times in advance.

Newtownbutler to Alderwood Bridge

21 miles (34km)

On this day's walk there are no shops, pubs or lodgings. Careful route finding is required along a maze of forest tracks. Alderwood Bridge is chosen as the end of this stretch so that you can head off-route to Fivemiletown for accommodation.

The Ulster Way heads along minor roads near Newtownbutler, then goes along a farm track to reach Ballagh Cross Roads. There's a settlement of sorts here, but many buildings are derelict. Note a glimpse of Armagh Manor as the trail leads towards a forest. Keep an eye peeled for waymarks at first, then good tracks lead from Coolnasillagh through Tully Forest. A rough path crosses from one minor road to another, then tracks are followed past Eshcleagh Lough and Lough Corry in Lisnaskea Forest.

There's a moorland interlude on the boggy slopes of Doocarn, where you need to take care across a rugged, hummocky moorland before descending to a valley. After a short road walk a farm track climbs uphill and a forest track leads past Lough Nadarra and Lough Jenkin to cross Jenkin Hill. Although the trail never reaches 300m during the day, some of the open views are extensive. A long and fiddly descent leads to a road, which runs down to Glenoo Bridge on the way out of Co Fermanagh. Follow a road near a forestry office and climb gently uphill before descending to Alderwood Bridge. If you're staying in nearby Fivemiletown, it's a good idea to ask someone to come out and collect you from this point, saving a long road walk into town.

SOUTHERN SECTION

Alderwood Bridge to Aughnacloy

21 miles (34km)

As you leave Alderwood Bridge, enjoy the next few forest tracks, as there are days of road walking ahead which are broken only by a very few paths and tracks. Quiet minor roads lead through Fardross Forest, then roads start climbing gradually uphill to leave the forests and lower pastures behind. The road frequently reaches 200m and passes a few houses in this broad, boggy country. A downhill stretch leads past Lough na Blaney Bane, locally called Lough Cavan, close to the border between Co Tyrone and Co Monaghan. Monaghan is the only one of Ulster's nine counties not touched

by the Ulster Way.

The road climbs over to Lough More, then there's a chance to walk through Altadaven Wood and have a look at St Patrick's Chair and Well. After walking down through the wood, minor roads lead to a main road near Favour Royal Forest. The trail doesn't go into the forest, though it is open to the public. The busy road is avoided by using quieter minor roads nearby. These eventually lead to Aughnacloy – a little town with an exceptionally wide main street. There are plenty of shops and pubs, but only limited lodgings.

Aughnacloy to Moy

23 miles (37km)

This is another long day of tarmac bashing, with only a couple of short stretches along paths. Basically, the Ulster Way follows the

River Blackwater, but there's little access to the riverside. The main road is followed out of Aughnacloy, but later a quieter minor road can be used between Crilly and Curlagh. You'll notice some fine buildings along the way, and see a little of the River Blackwater. There's food, drink and limited lodgings on offer in the planned estate village of Caledon. There are three large estates straddling the border in this area – Caledon, Tynan and Glaslough, in Co Tyrone, Co Armagh and Co Monaghan respectively. The boundary wall of the Caledon estate is followed, then the lovely Dredge Bridge – a suspension footbridge – can be crossed over the Blackwater. There's also a picnic site.

The Blackwater makes a pronounced change of direction at Caledon and the Ulster Way tries to follow it by using a series of minor roads. While walking along them, you'll catch a glimpse of an old canal from time to time.

The roads lead through Ballymacully and Wilsonstown to reach Milltown. At that point, the tow-path of the old canal can be used and riverside paths are available around Benburb. It's worth having a look round Benburb, taking in an old fortified bawn. There's also food, drink and accommodation if you want to break this long day's walk into two easier days.

Blackwatertown is just along the river from Benburb, and it also has useful facilities. Have a look at an old stone cross by the church. Follow narrow minor roads which have a view over the River Blackwater. These lead to Charlemont and a short walk off-route takes in Moy, which has shops, pubs and B & Bs available. Some of the buildings are arranged around a pleasant square.

Moy to Portadown

21 miles (34km)

Today's stretch of road walking can be broken fairly early with a walk around The Argory – a house and woodlands in the care of the National Trust. There's a short path alongside the River Blackwater, then you could later make a detour near a motorway to visit Peatlands Country Park. The Ulster Way passes this bogland by road, heading for the village of Maghery at the southern end of Lough Neagh, an enormous freshwater lake measuring over 150 square miles (400 sq km). Too big to see properly, its waters lap the shores of five counties.

Minor roads are a step back from the shore, and also later a step away from the River Bann, which is roughly traced to Portadown. The trail passes several farms and quite a few of the orchards which have earned Co Armagh the title of 'Orchard of Ireland'. Roads lead through the tiny village of Crabtreelane, across a motorway and finally into Portadown. This is a busy little town with a full range of services and good access to the River Bann.

Portadown to Newry

21 miles (34km)

A good, firm path is followed away from Portadown, along the bank of the River Bann. At the Reagh Bog there's a bridge which gives access to the tow-path of the Newry Canal. Although derelict, the canal usually carries some measure of water and at least the tow-path is walkable. It isn't yet officially part of the Ulster Way, but you'll welcome the break from tarmac bashing. The trail runs between the canal and a parallel railway, passing locks and bridges. You may find it easier to follow a short length of road into the village of Scarva, where you'll find a shop and pub.

Continuing along the canal, there's a glimpse of Lough Shark before Poyntzpass is reached.

Again, you could detour into town to avail yourself of its services. The tow-path is under tarmac on the walk away from Poyntzpass, but the path later leads on to the little village of Jerrettspass. Now the tow-path runs between the canal and a parallel main road, and this is the situation practically all the way to Newry. It's a well walked stretch, so you can put on a spurt of speed to end the day's walk. Newry has an excellent range of shops and pubs, and a very decorative cathedral, but not much accommodation. There are a few B & Bs in the countryside to the south of town, but off the course of the Ulster Way.

SOUTH EASTERN SECTION

Newry to Rostrevor

11 miles (18km)

The walk from Newry to Rostrevor is almost all along roads. It's an easy day's walk and quite short, but if you continue beyond Rostrevor you could have difficulty reaching Newcastle, which is the next place on the route with accommodation. The route leaves Newry with a steep climb uphill, offering good views across to Slieve Gullion and the Cooley Hills. There's a descent to cross a valley, then a climb from Greenan Lough over to

reedy Milltown Lough. A muddy track leads around the head of the lake, then roads are followed as high as 230m before running downhill to cross Moygannon River. There are fine views over Carlingford Lough to Carlingford Mountain as a high road is followed by Knockbarragh Park. A final descent leads to Rostrevor – an attractive little town with shops, pubs and accommodation available. There's a camp-site in a nearby forest.

Rostrevor to Newcastle

22 miles (36km)

This long day's walk across the northern slopes of the Mountains of Mourne starts with a series of easy tracks through Rostrevor Forest. There are occasional views over Kilbroney River, then the trail crosses Yellow Water River and runs through a narrow, forested valley between Crotlieve and Tievedockdarragh. Emerging from the forest there's a view along

Shanky's River and the trail leads across a bouldery hillside to pass a mass rock near another patch of forest. A stony track leads up into a high valley, then a rugged moorland gap has to be crossed to reach Rocky Water. A stream is followed up to a high gap where the formidable Batts Wall is found.

This very stout, solid wall leads steeply uphill

to the 559m summit of Slievemoughanmore which is the highest point gained by the Ulster Way. A descent to a gap is followed by a less steep climb to the 533m summit of Pigeon Rock Mountain. There are excellent views ahead to even higher mountains, but you'd need energy in abundance to cover those today. Batts Wall leads down to a road at Deers Meadow and a road is followed above Spelga Dam to reach the smaller Fofany Dam. A path leads down to this little reservoir, then the trail is routed along the hillside until it crosses Trassey River. Follow the river downstream and later use a series of forest tracks to get through Tollymore Forest Park. Keep an eye open for waymarks, as there are several junctions to be negotiated on the walk through the forest. Roads, tracks and paths finally lead down to Newcastle. This popular seaside resort has plenty of shops and pubs, and accommodation includes a youth hostel and nearby camp-sites.

Newcastle to Killough

19 miles (31km)

The walk from Newcastle to Dundrum follows the sandy beach around the Murlough Dunes. This area is managed as a nature reserve. When the tide is out you can walk on firm sand, but once round a point the sands become quite soft. Come ashore at a wooded area and cross the Downshire Bridge to reach Dundrum. You'll find food, drink and lodgings if you need them. A disused railway trackbed has been converted into a coastal footpath leading inland to Blackstaff Bridge.

The rest of the day's walk is along roads. A minor road runs through the village of Ballykinler, where there's a large army camp. After passing Tyrella House the Ulster Way follows the main coastal road through Minerstown to Murphystown and Rossglass. You may be able to break at a little pub along here. You could also take any of the beach roads and walk along stretches of the sandy or rocky shore to avoid the main road. A minor road is followed from Rossglass to Killough and if you've time you might visit a ruined church near St John's Point. Killough features plenty of fine old ruins and the town is well worth exploring. There are shops, pubs and a few B & Bs. If you have any difficulty finding a place to stay, then you could continue to Ardglass.

Killough to Strangford

13 miles (21km)

A simple road walk leads around Killough Harbour and Coney Island Bay to reach Ardglass. This is a pleasant little town built on a rocky inlet. When you leave town you can visit a ruined church on a low hill and enjoy the fine views of the surrounding countryside. The Mountains of Mourne will remain prominent in the view for most of the Ulster Way now. A minor road leaves the main road and a track later leads towards the shore and St Patrick's Well. An interesting coastal path follows the low cliff line to Ballyhornan, with Guns Island lying offshore. You can break for food and drink.

The rest of the day's walk is along roads. A minor road leads back to the main coastal road, where the little Kilclief Castle can be found. Some time could be spent studying seals at the Cloghy Rocks Nature Reserve. The seals have little to do but wait for the tide to bring fish through the turbulent narrows of Strangford Lough. The interesting little town of Strangford is soon reached. There is food and drink on offer, but if you're struggling to find a place to stay, catch the next ferry across the narrows of Strangford Lough to spend a night at Portaferry. The ferry runs from early until late and fills a gap in the main coastal road.

(overleaf) **A track leads above Shanky's River into the Mountains of Mourne**

Strangford to Killyleagh

20 miles (32km)

The town of Strangford and the neighbouring National Trust property of Castleward feature all sorts of fortifications, all obviously built to control the narrow tidal inlet. A coastal path can be followed as far as Audley's Castle, by which time Strangford Lough has opened into a wide, island-studded sea lough. The whole area is managed as a nature reserve and has a profuse birdlife. Stories of St Patrick abound and this particular area is even called St Patrick's Country. Although the good man's first experience of Ireland was slavery on Slemish in Co Antrim, he later landed at Strangford Lough and founded a church at nearby Saul. He travelled widely and had his capital at Armagh, but is believed to be buried at Downpatrick. The Ulster Way goes along a road below Slieve Patrick and on to Saul. A church has been built there in recent times, but to an ancient design. You could break at a pub for a while.

The trail continues along roads, then follows a path around the head of Quoile Pondage, a section of Strangford Lough which has been dammed to form a permanent freshwater lake. After this pleasant scene a main road is followed most of the way to Killyleagh. It passes Delamount Country Park, which you could explore. Just beyond Delamount there's a minor road down to the shore of Strangford Lough, reaching it at Nickey's Point. The trail runs towards the harbour at Killyleagh. There is food and drink to be had in town, but very little in the way of lodgings. If you can't find a place to stay, then catch a bus to Downpatrick for a wider range of services.

Killyleagh to Newtownards

21 miles (34km)

A large and splendid castle is passed on the way out of Killyleagh. Usually, the gate is left open even if the castle is closed to the public. The Ulster Way passes a shabby monument and climbs past an old mill pond. Minor roads avoid the main road and lead through low, rolling drumlin country with occasional wide views. There are odd visits to the shore of Strangford Lough. Quarterland Bay and Ballymorran Bay are followed by an interesting stretch of coastline between Whiterock and Sketrick Island. When you're high above the shore you'll see dozens of islands, plus many sandbanks at low water. After passing Ardmillan there's a climb uphill to follow a track which is muddy in places. More roads lead by way of Castle Espie to reach the outskirts of Comber. This little town is bypassed by Ulster Wayfarers, who can follow a stretch of disused railway trackbed to a busy road.

Farm tracks lead towards Scrabo Hill and a circuitous woodland path is finally followed by a climb to an enormous monumental tower. Enjoy the sweeping views which seem to take in most of the course of the Ulster Way. A steep descent leads to Newtownards and you head straight for the centre of town. There are some fine buildings, plenty of shops and pubs, but not a great number of places to stay. It's not generally realised that most brands of walking socks are actually knitted in Newtownards.

A view along a street of colourful houses in the little town of Ardglass

Castleward – a National Trust property on the shore of Strangford Lough

Newtownards to Holywood

13 miles (21km)

The climb above Newtownards is rather grim at first, passing a quarry and an old mining area. Once clear of all that, there are some pleasant woodland tracks. A road walk leads past a pub and the Clandeboye Estate. After crossing a very busy road, a minor road leads into the lovely village of Crawfordsburn. The oldest inn in Ireland is passed, if you want to take a break there. The trail goes down the pleasantly wooded Crawfordsburn Glen to reach the popular Crawfordsburn Country Park. The shore of Belfast Lough has been reached and this can be followed to Holywood. For most of the way, there's a good path, with only very slight diversions inland. Holywood is a busy little town with a range of shops, pubs and lodgings. Its most notable feature is a very tall, prominent and long established maypole at a busy road junction.

Holywood to Dunmurry

21 miles (34km)

After leaving Holywood, the trail wanders towards Redburn Country Park and climbs uphill for a fine view over Belfast Lough to the Antrim Mountains. A path leads gradually downhill and a series of roads lead through the suburbs of South Belfast. The trail runs fairly close to the parliament buildings at Stormont, but you'd need to make a detour to see them. A number of small shops are passed, if you need to buy anything. A track goes uphill from a church to join a road over Braniel Hill. The trail stays above the city for a while to reach Lisnabreeny. A path heads down to Lisnabreeny House, then another path zigzags down steps in the lovely, wooded Glencregagh to emerge on a busy road. The Ulster Way passes Belfast International Youth Hostel, if you want to break early.

Quiet paths lead into Belvoir Forest Park, where you can enjoy mixed woodlands and a variety of paths and tracks. There's a long stretch of the River Lagan to be followed, using a good, firm tow-path. Eventually, the wooded banks of the Lagan are left and the Ulster Way heads for Sir Thomas and Lady Dixon Park. This area is a mixture of gardens, parkland and woodland. After following a road across a motorway the trail ends back where it started – in Dunmurry. It's likely that some parts will eventually be re-routed away from the roads, making this long trail even longer.

ULSTER WAY INFORMATION

Schedule:	*miles*	*km*
Dunmurry – Whiteabbey BB	17	27
Whiteabbey – Ballynure BB	13	21
Ballynure – Glenarm BB	20	32
Glenarm – Cushendall YH	14	22
Cushendall – Ballycastle IH	20	32
Ballycastle – Portballintrae BB	19	31
Portballintrae – Castlerock BB	22	36
Castlerock – Formoyle for BB	17	28
Formoyle – Dungiven BB	22	36
Dungiven – Moneyneany BB	12	19
Moneyneany – Cranagh BB	14	22

Cranagh – Mountjoy BB	22	35
Mountjoy – Lough Bradan Forest for BB	24	38
Lough Bradan Forest – Pettigo BB	12	19
Pettigo – Rosscor BB	14	23
Rosscor – Doagh Glebe for BB	16	25
Doagh Glebe – Belcoo BB	16	25
Belcoo – Derrylinn BB	23	37
Derrylinn – Newtownbutler BB	13	21
Newtownbutler – Alderwood Bridge for BB	21	34
Alderwood Bridge – Aughnacloy BB	21	34
Aughnacloy – Moy BB	23	37
Moy – Portadown BB	21	34
Portadown – Newry BB	21	34
Newry – Rostrevor BB	11	18
Rostrevor – Newcastle YH	22	36
Newcastle – Killough BB	19	31
Killough – Strangford BB	13	21
Strangford – Killyleagh BB	20	32
Killyleagh – Newtownards BB	21	34
Newtownards – Holywood BB	13	21
Holywood – Dunmurry BB	21	34
Total distance	577	929

Maps:

OSNI 1:50,000 Discoverer Sheets 4, 5, 7, 8, 9, 12, 13, 15, 17, 18, 19, 20, 21, 26, 27 & 29.

Guidebooks:

No complete guide to the route, though a number of booklets and leaflets cover most parts and can be obtained from the Sports Council for Northern Ireland. Also useful is *Walking the Ulster Way*, by Alan Warner, published by Appletree Press Ltd.

Accommodation List:

An Information Guide to Accommodation for Walkers on the Ulster Way, published by the Northern Ireland Tourist Board.

Tourist Information Centres:

Belfast, Carnlough, Cushendall, Cushendun, Ballycastle, Giant's Causeway, Portrush, Portstewart, Coleraine, Castlerock, Cranagh, Omagh, Enniskillen, Armagh, Lurgan, Newry, Newcastle, Portaferry, Downpatrick, Newtownards, Bangor.

Appendix I - Future Trails

Here are details, or rather brief notes, of a dozen more trails which are being planned and will eventually join the official stable of state funded routes. Some are still being negotiated, while others are already partly waymarked, and one or two might just be opening as you're reading about them. Specific opening dates aren't always available, but look out for them from 1995 onwards.

England

Cotswold Way:
This trail is already a popular unofficial route and is well walked. It runs from Chipping Campden, over the Cotswold Hills, to the city of Bath.

Pennine Bridleway:
This route runs roughly parallel to the Pennine Way, but starts at Wirksworth and ends near Hexham. It's intended to be used by walkers, horse riders and cyclists.

Hadrian's Wall:
A short coast to coast route from the Tyne to the Solway shore which follows Hadrian's Wall wherever possible and visits other Roman sites. Already a popular choice among walkers.

Wales

Glyndwr's Way:
The route has already been waymarked, but will be upgraded to the status of a National Trail. It wanders around the mid-Wales county of Powys and links with the Offa's Dyke Path.

Scotland

Great Glen Way:
A trail running through the Great Glen of Scotland from Fort William to Inverness, using stretches of the Caledonian Canal tow-path, forest tracks and lakeside walks.

Ireland

Royal Canal:
A partly waymarked trail along the tow-path of the Royal Canal. Ultimately it should be possible to follow the canal from the outskirts of Dublin to the banks of the River Shannon.

Grand Canal:
A partly waymarked trail along the tow-path of the Grand Canal. Ultimately it should be possible to follow the canal from the outskirts of Dublin to the banks of the River Shannon.

Wexford Coastal Path:
A coastal trail is being developed around Co Wexford which will link with a short trail continuing around Dunmore East to Waterford city.

St Declan's Way:
A route commemorating St Declan's journey from the shore at Ardmore, over the Knockmealdown Mountains, to visit St Patrick at the celebrated Rock of Cashel.

Munster Way:
A route which has been partly waymarked and will ultimately run from Carrick-on-Suir to Killarney, linking the South Leinster Way with the Kerry Way and Beara Way.

Ballyhoura Way:
A partly waymarked trail running through the Ballyhoura Mountains. It will be extended piecemeal southwards to link with the Munster Way and northwards into the midlands.

Connemara Way:
A route through the striking landscape of Connemara, visiting the Connemara National Park and tying in with the course of the Western Way.

FORTHCOMING TRAILS

Appendix II – Useful Addresses

State Agencies Developing Trails

Countryside Commission
John Dower House
Crescent Place
Cheltenham
Gloucestershire
GL50 3RA

Countryside Council for Wales
Plas Penrhos
Ffordd Penrhos
Bangor
Gwynedd
LL57 2LQ

Scottish Natural Heritage
Battleby
Redgorton
Perth
PH1 3EW

Cospoir (National Sports Council)
11th Floor
Hawkins House
Dublin 2

Sports Council for Northern
Ireland
House of Sport
Upper Malone Road
Belfast
BT9 5LA

Ordnance Survey Offices

Ordnance Survey of Great Britain
Romsey Road
Maybush
Southampton
Hampshire
SO9 4DH

Ordnance Survey of Ireland
Phoenix Park
Dublin 8

Ordnance Survey of Northern
Ireland
Colby House
Stranmillis Court
Belfast
BT9 5BJ

Hostelling Organisations

Youth Hostels Association
(England & Wales)
Trevelyan House
8 St Stephens Hill
St Albans
Hertfordshire
AL1 2DY

Scottish Youth Hostels
Association
7 Glebe Crescent
Stirling
FK8 2JA

An Oige (Irish Youth Hostels
Association)
39 Mountjoy Square
Dublin 1

Youth Hostels Association of
Northern Ireland
56 Bradbury Place
Belfast
BT7 1RU

Independent Hostel Owners of
Ireland
Co-ordinator
Campus House
3 Woodland View
Western Road
Cork

Irish Approved Independent
Hostels
Doolin Hostel
Doolin Village
Co Clare

Path Associations

South West Way Association
Windlestraw
Penquit
Ermington
Ivybridge
Devon
PL21 0LU

Society of Sussex Downsmen
93 Church Road
Hove
East Sussex
BN3 2BA

Friends of the Ridgeway
90 South Hill Park
London
NW3 2SN

Peddars Way Association
150 Armes Street
Norwich
NR2 4EG

Offa's Dyke Association
Offa's Dyke Heritage Centre
West Street
Knighton
Powys
LD7 1EW

Pennine Way Association
Hon Secretary
29 Springfield Park Avenue
Chelmsford
Essex
CM2 6EL

Walking Organisations

Ramblers' Association
1/5 Wandsworth Road
London
SW8 2XX

Backpackers Club
PO Box 381
Reading
Berkshire
RG3 4RL

Long Distance Walkers'
Association
7 Ford Drive
Yarnfield
Stone
Staffordshire
ST15 0RP

Tourist Boards

English Tourist Board
Thames Tower
Blacks Road
Hammersmith
London
W6 9EL

Bwrdd Crocso Cymru (Welsh
Tourist Board)
Brunel House
2 Fitzalan Road
Cardiff
CF2 1UY

Scottish Tourist Board
23 Ravelston Terrace
Edinburgh
EH4 3EU

Bord Failte (Irish Tourist Board)
Baggot Street Bridge
Dublin 2

Northern Ireland Tourist Board
59 North Street
Belfast
BT1 1ND

Index